THE STORY OF THE WORLD

BOOK II.

THE DISCOVERY OF NEW WORLDS

FROM THE ROMAN EMPIRE TO THE RENAISSANCE
A.D. 4 TO SIXTEENTH CENTURY

JOAN OF ARC

THE DISCOVERY OF NEW WORLDS

BY

M. B. SYNGE

ILLUSTRATED BY E. M. SYNGE, A.R.E.

YESTERDAY'S CLASSICS

CHAPEL HILL, NORTH CAROLINA

This edition, first published in 2006 by Yesterday's Classics, is an unabridged republication of the work originally published by William Blackwood and Sons in 1903. For a full listing of books published by Yesterday's Classics, visit www.yesterdaysclassics.com. Yesterday's Classics is the publishing arm of the Baldwin Project which presents the complete text of dozens of classic books for children at www.mainlesson.com under the editorship of Lisa M. Ripperton and T. A. Roth.

ISBN-10: 1-59915-014-X
ISBN-13: 978-1-59915-014-7

Yesterday's Classics
PO Box 3418
Chapel Hill, NC 27515

CONTENTS

CHAPTER 1

THE ROMAN WORLD

"Let the great world spin for ever down the ringing
grooves of change."
—TENNYSON.

IN this new century, the story of the world was the story of Rome herself, for she ruled over nearly all the world that was known to the men of these olden times.

Let us remember that we are still talking of two thousand years ago, though we have almost unconsciously glided from the era known as B.C.— that is, Before Christ—to that known as A.D., Anno Domini, the year of our Lord.

It is sometimes hard to realise all that had happened before this time in the far-off ages of long ago. And yet it is all so interesting and so vastly important. It shows us how earnest work and toil raised each nation in turn to a high position, and how the acquisition of wealth or the greed of conquest brought that nation low.

We must now see how Rome too,—"Golden Rome," as she was called by the poets of her day,— the Mistress of the World, fell, owing to her desire for wealth and display, indolence and luxury, and how great and terrible was her fall.

While the child Christ was growing up in his quiet home in the East, Cæsar Augustus was still ruling the great Roman world, of which Rome itself was the centre. Augustus did what he could to make Rome, the capital of the whole world, worthy of her name.

Like Pericles at Athens in the olden days, he built beautiful buildings and tried to make the city as famous as possible. Many races met within her gates, many languages were spoken in her streets. Eastern princes and wildly-clad Britons and Gauls, low-browed Egyptians and sunburnt Spaniards,—all might have been seen at this time in the Forum at Rome, together with the Romans and Greeks.

Anxious to communicate with all parts of his mighty empire, Augustus started the imperial post. At certain stations along the great military roads, which now stretched from Rome to Cadiz in Spain, as well as to the coasts of France and Holland, he established settlements. Officers and messengers, with horses and mules, were ready to ride off, at a moment's notice, with messages from the emperor, to those who were ruling provinces under him. Along these great roads the legions of Rome were continually marching to and from the provinces, their tall helmets flashing in the sunlight as they tramped along the paved roads to protect the interests of Rome in distant lands.

The "Queen of Roman Roads," as it was called, was that known as the Appian Way, along which passed the traffic between Rome and the South, extending to Brindisi. It was a splendid road, broad enough for two carriages to pass one another, and built of hard stones hewn smooth.

Thus the countries dependent on Rome could pour their produce into the Golden City; while on the other hand the famous Augustan roads, starting from the golden milestone in the Forum,—the very heart of the Empire,—carried Roman civilisation and life to the western limits of Europe.

Then there were Roman possessions across the sea.

The whole northern coast of Africa was hers, from Carthage to Alexandria. Alexandria was at this time second only to Rome itself: as a centre for commerce she stood at the head of all the cities in the world.

Egypt supplied Rome with grain, which was shipped from Alexandria; the traffic of the East and West met in her streets; she had the finest Greek library in the world, and she was famous for her scholars and merchants.

But the reign of the emperor Augustus was drawing to its end. He was an old man now, and he had reigned over the empire forty-five years.

There had been peace throughout the latter part of his reign, disturbed only by one battle. This was in Germany, when the Germans won a victory over the consul Varus. It preyed on the mind of the old emperor, and he would sit grieving over it, at times beating his head against the wall and crying "Varus, Varus, give me back my legions."

He was never the same again. He set his empire in order and prepared for death.

"Do you think I have played my part well on the stage of life?" he asked those who stood round him, as he arranged his grey hair and beard before a mirror which he had called for.

Compared with those that came after, he had indeed played his part well. The Romans delighted to honor him. They called the sixth month in the Roman year, August, after him, just as they had called the month before, July, after Julius Cæsar, and these names have lasted to this very day.

CHAPTER 2

A GREAT WORLD POWER

"God's in His Heaven,
All's right with the world."
—BROWNING.

EVENTS which affect us to-day were now crowding thickly together. The Emperor Augustus Cæsar was dead. Tiberius Cæsar ruled the great empire of the Roman world, including distant Judæa, where Jesus Christ was living out His quiet life, teaching a new order of things to those who would hear.

But the Jews—those direct descendants of Abraham the patriarch, who had long ago migrated from Chaldea to the land of Canaan,—the Jews were looking for a great earthly conqueror. They had refused to acknowledge the claims of Christ to be that conqueror, and they wished to bring about His death as soon as possible.

"What thinkest thou?" they said one day—"Is it lawful to give tribute to Cæsar, or not?"

"Show Me the tribute money," answered Christ.

And they brought Him a penny, a Roman penny made of silver, worth about sevenpence-halfpenny of present money.

"Whose is this image and superscription?" He asked them.

"Cæsar's," was their answer.

Then saith He unto them: "Render therefore unto Cæsar the things which are Cæsar's; and to God the things which are God's."

This was no earthly conqueror like the Cæsars, whom they could expect to give them high places, to restore to them their rights and exalt them above their fellows. This Man taught that the world must be a great brotherhood, bound together by peace and love. And the Jews put Him to death, crucifying Him, according to their eastern custom.

They had killed Him when He was yet young, but they could not kill His teaching. Under His disciples and apostles it spread rapidly.

"Go ye into all the world and preach the Gospel (good news) to every creature."

These had been among the last commands given to the followers of Christ. Among the first to carry out this great command of his Master was Paul.

The first city he chose in which to preach was Antioch—"Antioch the Beautiful," or the Crown of the East, as the men of old called the city. North of Tyre and Sidon, on the sea-coast of Syria, it stood, on the great trade-road between Ephesus and the

East. Here were men from Cyprus and men from Cyrene, here lived numbers of wealthy Romans and Greeks. It was a good place to which to carry the good news. In a year's time Paul had taught many people, and here the name of "Christian" was first given to those who followed the teaching of Christ.

Tiberius the emperor was dead, and Claudius Cæsar was ruling over the Roman Empire; but the new teaching in far-away Antioch had not yet penetrated into the heart of Rome, though the sayings of the Master had been written down in the four books still known as the Gospels.

From Antioch St Paul crossed over to Cyprus, the island to which the Phœnicians had made their first voyage across the seas, and which now belonged to Rome.

After a time he set sail for the mainland of Asia Minor.

Asia Minor was indeed the highway by which Christianity passed to the capital of the world. Travelling from town to town, mainly along the great caravan routes of the country, the faithful apostle reached the sea-coast near the old town of Troy.

Here one night he had a dream. A man of Macedonia, in the bright clothing of that nation, appeared to him.

"Come over into Macedonia and help us," he said.

Paul could not resist such an appeal. Setting sail, he crossed over to Macedonia, setting foot for the first time on European soil. From thence he passed south to Athens, once the most beautiful city in the world.

Here he would see the great statue of the goddess Athene crowning the Acropolis. He knew how corrupt the city had grown since the brilliant times of Pericles, and "his spirit was stirred in him, when he saw the city wholly given to idolatry."

Standing on Mars Hill, a lofty rock rising from the very heart of the city, with the clear blue sky of Greece above him, he spoke to the men of Athens from the very depths of his heart.

Again and again we find him travelling from town to town, standing amidst temples and "idols made with hands," and telling the people of the Master he would have them serve instead. At Ephesus, where, glittering in brilliant beauty, stood the great temple of Diana, Paul nearly lost his life in the uproar that followed his plain speaking. But he was ready to die for the Master if need be. Again preaching at Jerusalem, tumults arose which ended in his imprisonment and his well-known trial.

"I stand at Cæsar's judgment-seat, where I ought to be judged," he said, appealing to the highest tribunal in the land. "I appeal unto Cæsar."

"Hast thou appealed unto Cæsar? Unto Cæsar shalt thou go," cried Festus, ruler of the province.

CHAPTER 3

VOYAGE AND SHIPWRECK

"Men that have hazarded
their lives for the name of
our Lord Jesus Christ."

—ACTS XV. 26.

To appeal to the great Roman Cæsar the apostle
Paul now set sail for his longest voyage. A convoy of
prisoners was starting for Rome, and with them Paul
embarked at Cæsarea, a new Roman seaport named
after Cæsar: with a fair wind the ship soon reached
Sidon. It was the last city on the coast of Syria he
ever saw.

Leaving Sidon, the old Phœnician port, the
wind blew from the north-west and drove them to

9

the north of the island of Cyprus. Still beating against a contrary wind, the ship reached the shores of Asia Minor, and put into the port of Myra, one of the great harbours of the Egyptian service. Here was a ship carrying corn from Alexandria to Rome, a large merchant vessel, which had probably been blown out of her course and taken refuge at Myra. On board this ship Paul and the prisoners were put, and off they sailed once more. Slowly they sailed south against heavy winds and high seas till they reached Crete, where in the harbour, which is known as "Fair Havens" to this day, they anchored to wait for a change of wind.

Time passed, and they were still wind-bound: autumn was coming on, and it was time for navigation in the Mediterranean to cease. The old ships were not fit to brave the storms of winter in the open sea. A discussion took place as to whether they should winter in Crete or push on farther. The owner of the ship was for going on: Paul advised caution.

"Sirs," he said, "I perceive that this voyage will be with hurt and much damage, not only of the cargo and ship, but also of our lives."

In spite of this advice, however, they determined to make for a safer harbour in which to spend the winter. With a south wind blowing softly they set sail, and had neared their desired haven, when a sudden violent wind came down from the mountains of Crete and struck the ship, whirling her round so that steering became impossible. An ancient ship with one huge sail was exposed to extreme danger from such a blast as now blew. The straining of the great sail on the single mast was more than the hull could bear, and the ship might any moment founder in the open sea.

The hurricane blew her southwards, away from Crete, and towards the dreaded quicksands of the African coast near Cyrene.

The violence of the storm continued. After drifting helplessly at the mercy of the wind and waves for two days and nights, they began to throw overboard the cargo to lighten the ship, and then "with our own hands," says the writer of the Acts, "we threw away all the ship's fittings and equipment."

Here is a striking picture of the growing panic. Still the wind blew, no sun shone by day, no stars lit the dark sea by night; cold and wet and very hungry, they drifted on towards death and destruction.

At last Paul made his voice heard above the storm. "Sirs, ye should have hearkened to my counsel, and not have set sail from Crete," he said; "thus you would have been spared this harm and loss. And now I exhort you to be of good cheer: for there shall be no loss of any man's life among you, but only of the ship."

The gale continued day and night for fourteen days. At the end of that time, towards midnight, the sailors heard the breaking of waves on a shore.

They were nearing land, but the danger was still great, for the ship might be dashed on the rocks and go to pieces. In an agony of terror they waited for the dawn. No coast was visible, only a wild waste of waters. The sailors, under pretext of casting anchors, lowered a boat, intending to row off and leave the sinking ship and its two hundred and seventy-six passengers to their fate. Paul saw their intention.

"Except these abide in the ship, ye cannot be saved," he said to those in authority. They had learnt to listen to the words of this remarkable prisoner. The ropes of the boat were instantly cut, and the sailors' selfish plan failed.

"This is the fourteenth day that you watch and continue fasting, and have taken nothing. Wherefore I beseech you to take some food: for this is for your safety."

Again Paul's advice was taken. Daylight came, land was visible, and they made for a pebbly beach and ran the ship aground. By means of boards and broken planks they all reached land safely, while the old ship which had borne them through the storm went to pieces before their eyes.

They had reached Malta, and the bay where they landed is known to-day as St Paul's Bay. The sight of the ship attracted the natives on the island—Phœnician and Greek settlers, subject now to Rome—and they treated the shipwrecked crew with unusual kindness.

For three months, until February opened the sea again to navigation, they stayed at Malta. Then another corn-ship from Alexandria—the "Castor and Pollux"—took the passengers on board, and sailed for Syracuse in Sicily. Here they waited three days for a good wind, which carried them through the narrow straits of Messina, dividing Italy from Sicily. They passed between chains of snow-clad hills, till at last the merchant ship sailed into a beautiful calm blue bay to unload its cargo, and very soon Paul found himself in the great city of Rome herself.

He had already sent a long letter or epistle to the men of Rome.

"I long to see you," he had written to them three years before this; "I am ready to preach the Gospel to you that are in Rome also."

Now he was among them. True, he was a prisoner: a light chain fastened his hand to that of a soldier who was guarding him, though he had his own house in the city.

And here Paul preached the good news he had brought, and the Romans became Christians in such numbers that they were recognised in the city by the emperor.

CHAPTER 4

THE TRAGEDY OF NERO

"Butchered to make a Roman holiday."
—BYRON.

MANY changes had taken place in Rome since the days of Tiberius Cæsar, who died four years after the crucifixion of Christ. The last of the Cæsars was now reigning in the person of one Nero. So far his youth had not been uneventful. When he was nine years old the Romans kept the great festival of the foundation of Rome. For eight and a half centuries their city had been growing in strength and importance. The last great deed had been the conquest of Britain, after which the emperor had named his little son, Britannicus.

An account of this festival has come down to us. In the great amphitheatre African lions, leopards, and tigers were hunted by Roman officers; gladiators contended with lions, and bulls fought; but one of the chief objects of interest was the appearance of the two little Cæsars, Nero and Britannicus, dressed in military uniforms richly gilt. Britannicus was but six, while Nero was nine, but the two little fellows took part in a sham fight between the Greeks and the defenders of Troy. The Romans took a great fancy to the boy Nero; and his mother, Agrippina, a very powerful lady, determined that he should be emperor.

When Nero was fourteen another great triumph took place in Rome. The emperor and his wife, Agrippina, sat on two thrones to watch, with the rest of Rome, the captives from Britain led through the streets.

The story about Caractacus, the warrior British chieftain, is well known. He stood before the Roman emperor. It was the custom at a triumph to kill the captives. The other prisoners had pleaded for their lives, but the island chief was proud. Standing before the imperial throne, he spoke fearlessly to the great Cæsar.

"If to my high birth and distinguished rank I had added the virtues of moderation, Rome had beheld me rather as a friend than a captive. I had arms and men and horses, I possessed extraordinary riches: can it be any wonder that I was unwilling to lose them? Because you Romans aim at extending your rule over all mankind, must all men cheerfully submit to your yoke? I am now in your power: if you take my life, all is forgotten; spare me, and as long as I live I shall praise your forgiveness."

> "He ceased; from all around upsprung
> A murmur of applause,
> For well had truth and freedom's tongue

Maintained their holy cause.
The conqueror was the captive then;—
He bade the slave be free again."

So ends the story: the chains that bound Caractacus were removed, and he passed away from the staring throng of Romans, repeating his gratitude for the emperor's generosity.

When Nero was seventeen he became emperor of the Roman Empire, now larger than it had ever been before, while his mother Agrippina was made regent. For the first few years of his reign all went well. He was a joyous boy, enjoying his life to the full. Chariot-driving was his delight. Even when a child he had a little ivory chariot with horses, as a toy to drive along on the polished surface of the marble table.

But soon he became cruel and revengeful. When he was eighteen he determined on the death of Britannicus, lest he should try to win the empire for himself. The story says that he had poison mixed under his own eyes, and made trial of it first on a pig; then he poisoned Britannicus. The boy died at once.

Wanting to marry a wife to whom Agrippina strongly objected, he determined that his mother must die. A ship was built that would suddenly open in the middle and plunge her, unawares, into the sea. This ship he presented to her himself. It was a splendid-looking galley, with sails of silk. Kissing her passionately, Nero handed her on board. The night

16

Nero and Britannicus

was warm and dark, though the sky was thick with stars, and the ship glided silently through the waters; till suddenly a signal rang out, and crash went the roof of the cabin, which was weighted with lead.

Agrippina found herself in the water; she struck out for the shore and was picked up by some fishermen. When Nero heard what had happened he was wild with rage, and by his orders she was stabbed to death. Then he married a wife who thought more of keeping good her complexion by bathing daily in asses' milk, than of helping her headstrong husband in the management of his vast empire. Luxury, cruelty, and banqueting were the order of the day, and Nero the emperor was the main actor in the coming tragedy.

CHAPTER 5

THE GREAT FIRE IN ROME

"Darkening the golden roof of Nero's world,
From smouldering Rome the smoke of ruin curled."
—WM. WATSON.

IT has been said, and perhaps it is true, that the emperor was mad at times and not responsible for all he did. Be this as it may, the year 64 was marked by a terrible fire in Rome, which lasted nearly a week and left a great part of Rome in ashes.

The summer had been hot and dry. One warm night in July a fire broke out in some wooden sheds where were stored quantities of spices, oil, and other materials likely to feed the flames. It has been said that the emperor himself set the city on fire in his mad rage; and that, posted on one of the highest points of Rome, dressed in one of his dramatic costumes, he took his lyre, and chanted the verses of Homer on the burning and destruction of Troy.

Here is the account from one of the old historians, Tacitus:—

"All was in the wildest confusion. Men ran hither and thither: some sought to extinguish the conflagration, some never heard that their houses were on fire till they lay in ashes. All shrieked and cried—men, women, children, old folks—in one vast confusion of sound, so that nothing could be distinguished for the noise, as nothing could be seen clearly for the smoke. Some stood silent and in despair, many were engaged in rescuing their possessions, whilst others were hard at work plundering. Men quarrelled over what was taken out of the burning houses, while the crush swayed this way and that way.

"Whilst this was going on at different points, a wind arose and spread the flames over the whole city. No one any longer thought of saving goods and houses, none now lamented their individual losses: all wailed over the general ruin and lamented the fate of the commonwealth."

The treasures gained in the East, the beautiful works of the Greek artists—statues, pictures, temples,—all were gone. A few shattered ruins stood up from among the ashes, and that was all.

Whispers that Nero had lit this fire grew loud. The emperor trembled. The guilt must be laid on some one. Why not on the Christians, who refused to take part in the emperor's riots and plays, his feasts and banquets. They were regarded with suspicion: they would be better away. As they had burned the city, argued the emperor, they themselves should be burned.

At the head of the Christians in Rome Paul was now working with his fellow-apostle Peter. He had toiled hard during his two years' residence in the great city, where the people had lost their ideals, lost their old love of freedom for their state, and lapsed into that condition of ease and luxury which, sooner or later, brings every nation to its fall. Paul was an old man now. His appeal to Nero had been successful, and he had been set at liberty. Here he had written his letters to the men of Ephesus (or the Ephesians),—beautiful letters, sad yet full of hope.

Again and again he repeated his charge to the brethren; they must carry on the work. His own end was near, his fight was nearly fought, his course was nearly finished. The end was now come.

One night a great show was announced by Nero to be held in the circus, within the gardens of the Imperial palace, at the foot of the Vatican Hill. It was summer time, and the Roman people crowded to take their places in the circus, now lit up by the flaming torches. The arena was full of stakes to which were tied human beings—Christians— wrapped in cloths of tow steeped in pitch. While these living torches flared and the shrieks of the martyrs rose above the noise of the music, Nero appeared dressed in green, in an ivory chariot, and drove on the gold sand round the circus.

But this was more than the Romans could endure, and, moved to pity, they begged that the dreadful spectacle should cease.

In this first persecution of the Christians it is said that both Paul and Peter suffered martyrdom in some form or other. Paul, as a Roman citizen, was beheaded; Peter was crucified, as his Master had been before him.

A great revulsion of feeling now set in against Nero. Such tyranny must end in disgrace. As time went on, one by one deserted him: courtiers, slaves, freedmen, all forsook him. At last the very guards at his palace left their post, and he made up his mind to flee from Rome. He could find no one to fly with him.

"Is it so hard to die?" said one man, quoting the poet Virgil.

"I have neither friend nor foe left," wailed Nero, when the gladiator he had ordered to kill him failed to do it.

It was night, a hot summer night, when the wretched emperor disguised himself and rode forth to seek a hiding-place, where at any rate his life might be safe. Summer lightning was flashing over the Alban Hills: it lit up the road before the flying emperor. He shivered with fear. As the morning dawned he was persuaded to creep into a villa owned by a freedman, Phaon. Through a hole at the back he crawled on all-fours, and threw himself on a miserable pallet inside.

A messenger rushed in with a letter. Nero snatched it from his hand and tore it open. He had been declared an enemy of the state, and was sentenced to die a traitor's death.

He must die now. Again and again he strove to nerve himself for the last effort, but it was not till the sound of the horses' hoofs was heard that he put the dagger to his throat.

So died Nero, the last of the Cæsars!

CHAPTER 6

THE DESTRUCTION OF POMPEII

"Those streets which never, since the days of yore,
By human footstep had been visited."

—SOUTHEY.

IN the days of the Emperor Titus a catastrophe, among the most awful in ancient history, occurred under the still smoking mountain of Vesuvius. For suddenly, without note or warning, two entire cities—Pompeii and Herculaneum—were wiped from the face of the earth. They were buried alive, and the people perished as they were pursuing their daily work and pleasure, by the eruption of the volcano in their midst. "Day was turned into night and light into darkness: an inexpressible quantity of dust and ashes was poured out, deluging land, sea, air, and burying two entire cities, while the people were sitting in the theatre." So writes an old historian.

Pompeii was an old town near the sea-coast of southern Italy, in a beautiful region under the shadow of Mount Vesuvius. It had been a Greek colony in the old days, when the Greeks occupied most of this part. But at this time—79 A.D.—it had been a Roman colony for some twenty-four years, and was a favourite resort of the Romans. It was a miniature Rome, with its tiny palaces, its forum, its theatre, its circus; a miniature Rome, too, in its luxury, its indolence, its very corruption. Crowded in the glassy bay outside were ships of commerce, and gilded galleys for the pleasure of the rich citizens, while the tall masts of the Roman fleet under the command of Pliny could be seen afar off.

It was the 23rd of November, and the afternoon was wearing on, when from the top of Vesuvius rose a lofty column of black smoke which, after rising high into the air, spread itself out into a cloud in the shape of a giant pine-tree. As the afternoon advanced the cloud increased in size and density, while the mountain cast up ashes and red-hot stones.

Panic-stricken, the inhabitants fled from the city, knowing not which way to turn. By this time the earth was trembling beneath them, and shock after shock of earthquake rent the ground. Darkness now came on, and all through that long black night the terror-stricken people must have made their way towards the seashore and along the coast. The account of these days has come to us, vivid in detail, from the pen of Pliny, who was an eyewitness of the whole thing, and whose uncle, commanding the Roman fleet at the time, died, suffocated by the vapour and flames from the burning mountain.

"Though it was now morning," says Pliny, who was with his mother some fourteen miles from the doomed city of Pompeii, "the light was exceedingly faint and languid. The buildings all around us tottered, and there was a great risk of our being overwhelmed. Then at last we decided on leaving the town. The mass of the inhabitants followed us, terror-stricken, pressing on us and pushing us forwards with their crowded ranks. When we got beyond the buildings we stopped in the midst of a most dangerous and dreadful scene. The sea seemed to roll back upon itself as if driven from its banks by the quaking of the earth, while a black and dreadful cloud, broken by zig-zags of flame, darted out a long train of fire like flashes of lightning, only much larger. The ashes now began to fall upon us. I turned my head and observed behind us a thick smoke, which came rolling after us like a torrent.

"Meanwhile the cloud descended and covered land and sea with a black darkness.

" 'Save yourself,' now begged Pliny's mother, thinking this was the end. 'I am old and content to die, provided I am not the cause of your death too.'

" 'I will only be saved with you,' answered young Pliny, taking her hand and urging her onwards."

Another shower of ashes and a dense mist now closed them in, and soon night came on. They could hear the shrieks of the women, the children crying for help, and the shouts of the men through the darkness. Ashes and fire still rained down upon them, until at last the dreary night was over. Day dawned; the sun shone faintly through the murky atmosphere, showing the whole country lying under a thick coating of white ashes, as under deep snow.

Though a great number of people escaped, some two thousand were buried by the ashes that completely covered the whole town. For the next fifteen hundred years the buried cities lay wrapped in sleep, their very existence forgotten, their site undiscovered.

Then, in the sixteenth century, a great Italian engineer built an aqueduct right through the ruins of Pompeii. But it was not till two hundred years later that any real discovery took place. Then, by royal orders, men began to dig out the buried ruins of the old towns of Pompeii and Herculaneum. From that day to this digging has gone on at intervals, until now we know just what the old town was like. We can walk over the old streets along which the Romans walked before ever this terrible catastrophe came upon them.

Here, to-day, may be seen the old buildings, houses and villas with paintings on the walls. They are as fresh as if done but yesterday: here are their pavements of mosaic, their baths, their shops, their temples, and the eight gates by which the old city is entered. The streets are very narrow, and it is clear that only one chariot could pass at a time. Still may be seen the marks of the chariot-wheels, crossing and recrossing each other in the few broad streets, but worn into ruts in the narrow ones.

But perhaps most startling of all the strange things to be seen in this old city of the dead past are the very old Romans themselves. Overtaken suddenly in the midst of life, they were covered with the burning ashes, which hardened on them, encasing the human figure and preserving it through the long ages.

So we see them, lying in the museum which stands at the entrance to the town. Mostly they lie in attitudes of terror, some with a hand across their eyes as if to hide out the dreadful sight, some on the point of flight, having hastily taken off their outer clothing. One girl has yet a ring on her finger, while there is a dog still lying as he lay seventeen hundred years before. As a German poet has said—

"The earth with faithful watch has hoarded all."

The unearthing of Pompeii has revealed much of the ancient habits and customs of the Romans of old in their pleasure-loving days. It has taught us about their houses, their amusements, their clothes, their food. Here are their bake-houses, their loaves of bread, their money, their ornaments; and as we stand in the now deserted streets, looking up to the treacherous mountain above, and away to the blue bay on the other side, we can realise what the old Roman life must have been.

CHAPTER 7

MARCUS AURELIUS

"The most beautiful figure in history."
—MATTHEW ARNOLD.

FROM time to time in the history of the world men have stood out, one by one, head and shoulders above their fellows,—men whose names can never perish, men whose acts will never die.

Such an one was Marcus Aurelius, emperor of the Roman Empire, but known to history as a great high-minded thinker, a pagan philosopher, true and firm and good in every action and every thought.

His life was not very full of incident: other men have done more and lived through stormier times than did Marcus Aurelius.

As a little boy he came under the notice of the Emperor Hadrian, who made the little Marcus a knight at the age of six. The "most true," he used to call the child, who even at this time was serious and thoughtful and noted for his truthfulness. Though delicate in health, his mother could not induce him to sleep on a bed spread with sheepskin, so Spartan was he in his ideas and so anxious to avoid being luxurious and indulgent. He was a Stoic—that is to say, he followed the teaching of a philosopher who lived long ago in Athens. This philosopher used to teach in a painted porch in that city, and *stoa* being the Greek for porch, his followers got the name of Stoics.

At twelve years old he adopted the dress of plain woollen stuff worn by the Stoics. He loved history, he clung to old forms and customs. And so the boy grew up in the heart of Rome with his high standard of duty, his indifference to pleasure and pain, his love of virtue, his simple outlook on life.

Hadrian the emperor had adopted him as his successor.

Marcus Aurelius had already shown himself able and capable in affairs of state. He was made consul at the age of seventeen; he had prepared well for the day when the responsibilities of the great world-empire should be his.

"Modestly take, cheerfully resign." These words were among his sayings, given to the world fourteen hundred years after his death.

He accepted his great empire with modesty, insisting on sharing it with his adopted brother Verus. Insurrection breaking out in a distant part of the huge Roman possessions, Marcus Aurelius sent Verus to quell it. But the legions employed in this war brought back to Rome the germs of a terrible pestilence, which had followed them along their line of march. The plague that now broke out devastated vast districts of the mighty empire, and carried off thousands of victims in Rome itself. Following the plague came a fire, and following the fire came an earthquake. Then disturbances arose on the Danube, calling forth the strength of the empire to repress them. It required all the stoical patience that Marcus Aurelius could command to stand firmly at the helm and steer through these storms—storms which, though he knew it not, were the beginning of the decline and fall of his great empire.

But duty called him from Rome and from home to the long exile of the camp. He was no soldier, but the fate of Rome hung on his presence with the soldiers in the field, and his resolution was staunch. He hated war; but the empire must be defended, and he readily exposed himself to eight winter campaigns on the frozen banks of the Danube. Here, amid the harsh and uncongenial surroundings of war, the great philosopher-emperor wrote his wonderful Thoughts, or Meditations as they are called.

Very pathetic are these great thoughts, tinged with a sadness which came from the hopelessness of his pagan philosophy. Life's day had been toilsome, the evening-tide was very lonely. Wasted with disease from camp life, his spirit broken by the death of his wife and four sons, he waits for the retreat to sound—waits for that death which he knows to be "rest."

"Come quickly, death, for fear I too forget myself," he cries, as he grows weaker and more suffering.

"Live as on a mountain. Let men see, let them know a real man, who lives as he was meant to live."

He had indeed lived on a mountain, lived his simple good life with the eyes of the whole world looking on him, and he had shown how it was possible to lead a grand life in the midst of a corrupt age.

His end was as his life had been—deliberate, unflinching, resolute. The habit of duty struggled with his failing body. His friends gathered round him. "Why weep for me?" he says in a passionless farewell; "think of the army and its safety: I do but go on before. Farewell."

Away from home, at Vienna, on the 17th of March 180, Marcus Aurelius died. Rome forgot the emperor in the man.

"Marcus, my father! Marcus, my brother! Marcus, my son!" cried the bereaved citizens, while Romans whispered to one another, "He whom the gods lent us has rejoined the gods."

Stoically this man had lived, stoically he died. At a time when national virtue was dead he had stood firm and true; but it was impossible for one man to stem the tide of Roman decline. And the centuries still turn to him for wisdom, and the Thoughts will ever remain imperishable, "dignifying duty, shaming weakness, and rebuking discontent."

So he stands from out the ages of the past—
"wise, just, self-governed, tender, thankful,
blameless, yet with all this, agitated, stretching out
his arms for Something beyond."

CHAPTER 8

DECLINE OF THE ROMAN EMPIRE

"And when Rome falls—the World."
—BYRON.

THE golden days of the great world-empire were now over. With the death of Marcus Aurelius her happiness and prosperity seemed to be gone for ever. She had reached the height of her glory. She had stretched her strong arms over land and sea— over Europe, Asia, and Africa; she had carried civilisation into the farthest limits of the known world, and now her power was ending. Other nations were to rise and play their part in the world's history.

Ten centuries had passed away since those days when Romulus with his small band of shepherds had fortified himself near the banks of the Tiber. During the first four ages the Romans, in the school of poverty, had learnt and practised that virtue which is the strength of nations. Patriotic, industrious, and courageous, they enlarged their boundaries, and for three hundred years they had lived in prosperity.

But for the last three hundred years they had been slowly but surely declining. Wealth had poured into their capital; Africans, Gauls, Britons, and Spaniards had lived in their midst; their old simplicity had gone, their spirit was broken, their old vigour had fled. The stern old Roman nature was softened by luxury, enfeebled by wealth, and the outlying peoples of the north were not slow to mark the growing weakness of the empire.

Marcus Aurelius had left a son who was in every way unworthy of his high-minded father. Under him the decline which had already begun went on apace. The empire was put up to auction. One ruler after another rose and fell. Under the African ruler Severus hope flickered up again. He was alive to the dangers of his country, and saw the need for closer union of the various provinces. He spent his time away from Rome, connecting the vast empire by a network of paved roads, which cut through hills and bridged over valleys and rivers. But Severus died at York on his way south from Scotland, and with his unworthy successors hope died away again.

For the next hundred years, emperor after emperor lived and died. But none was great enough or good enough to save the Empire, now tottering more rapidly to its fall; for the people are the backbone of their country, and the Roman people had lost their old spirit.

Under Diocletian, a soldier risen from the ranks, who was hailed as emperor by the people, the great Empire was divided into two parts. One man was to rule the East and another the West, while each ruler was to select his successor. For twenty years he ruled, and then he made up his mind to give up the responsibilities of empire and retire to private life.

On the 1st of May, in the year 305, a vast number of troops assembled on a great plain beyond the Danube. On a knoll in the midst a throne was erected, on which the emperor sat in the sight of all. Before the gazing crowds he took off his purple robe, his jeweled crown, his imperial ornaments, and put them on his successor. Then descending into the plain he mounted his chariot, drove once more through the streets and away to his seaside palace.

Once, later on, when things were going ill, Diocletian was urged to come out of his retreat and take upon him the purple again, but his answer was ever the same: "Come and look at the cabbages I have planted."

While the Emperor Diocletian was still reigning, a young boy about sixteen, son of the man whom he had elected to succeed him, was growing up to "command the admiration of all who beheld him." Already he had shown himself able and clever. "No one," says the enthusiastic historian, "was comparable to him for grace and beauty of person, or height of stature and greatness of strength."

This was the future Constantine the Great, who was to take a great step in the history of the world by making a new capital for the Roman Empire, known to us to-day as Constantinople.

While Diocletian was growing cabbages in his country home, Constantine and his colleague ascended the thrones of the East and West. But it was not for long. After a civil war, Constantine became sole emperor.

He will ever be remembered in history for the mighty change he accomplished in the world's religion by becoming a Christian. There is an old story which tells how he decided on this change, from his pagan worship of the Roman gods to his worship of the God preached by Paul in Rome more than two hundred years before.

He was going to battle on the banks of the Tiber, says the story. Suddenly there appeared before the whole army a bright cross of light in the noonday sky, with the words plainly traced round it: "In this sign shalt thou conquer."

That night, when he lay down to sleep, the Christ appeared to Constantine in a vision, with the same sign which he had already seen. He commanded him to make a standard with that sign of the cross upon it, and he should have victory over his enemies.

The following day the soldiers went into battle with the sacred sign on their shields; they fought under the standard of the cross and won the battle. And Constantine entered Rome—a Christian.

CHAPTER 9

CHRISTIANS TO THE LIONS

"Follow the Christ, the King;
Live pure, speak true, right wrong; follow the King."
—Tennyson.

NOW that an emperor of the Roman Empire had for the first time become a Christian, it will be interesting to note what had been happening with regard to the band of Christians in Rome since the days when St Paul and St Peter had suffered martyrdom more than two hundred years before.

Persecution had only served to spread the faith which the followers of Christ would sooner die than give up. Before long little bands of Christians were to be found in many of the cities under Rome. At Antioch, at Alexandria, at Carthage there were large numbers.

Let us see by the lives and deaths of a few of these, what firm root the new faith had taken. In the days of the Emperor Trajan, away in Antioch there lived a Christian bishop called Ignatius. When the emperor had won his victory over the Dacians he ordered that sacrifice should be offered to the gods in all the provinces of his vast empire. Ignatius and the Christians in Antioch refused. Trajan ordered that Ignatius should be brought before him, and reproved him for keeping the people from the temples of the gods.

"O Cæsar," answered Ignatius, "wert thou to offer me all the treasures of thy empire, yet would I not cease to adore the only true and living God."

When Trajan heard this he commanded that Ignatius's mouth should be stopped and that he be cast into a dungeon. At first he settled that the bishop should be put to death at once; then he ordered that he should be sent to Rome and reserved for the amphitheatre. Weeping and kissing his garments and his chains, the Christians of Antioch saw Ignatius depart in a ship bound for Rome. There he was led forth into the amphitheatre, where two furious lions were let loose upon him, tearing him to pieces, till nothing was left but a few bones.

Under Marcus Aurelius the persecutions of the Christians still went on, while under his successors it was yet more rigorously pursued.

Some fifty years before the rule of Diocletian there lived at Carthage a bishop called Cyprian, who was the most important Christian in the whole of North Africa. Carthage had been rebuilt since the old days, when the Roman conquerors had burnt the ships in the harbour so dear to the conquerors of the sea: it was now a beautiful city with white walls and houses shining by the blue waters of the

Mediterranean, rich in temples, gardens, and palm trees. Here, then, Cyprian laboured and taught; here was a strong band of Christians under him, so strong indeed that one of the emperors ordered a wholesale persecution of them.

"Cyprian to the lions" cried the excited crowd of pagans in the city, anxious to please the severe emperor. But Cyprian felt he could serve his cause best by living yet a little, so he took refuge in flight.

Eight years later, he was to show that he was no coward, but ready and willing to die for the faith if need be. The eyes of North Africa were upon him. He knew that an order had gone forth for the execution of all Christian teachers. The Bishop of Carthage knew, too, that he would be among the first to die. He was in his garden when the officers came to take him before his Roman judge. They placed him between them in the chariot and drove to a private house in the town. A supper was prepared for him and his friends. The streets outside were filled with anxious crowds passing to and fro. The next morning found him before the judge. He was commanded to offer sacrifice to the Roman gods. He firmly refused. The sentence of death was pronounced. As it reached the listening crowds of Christians waiting outside, a general cry arose from the heart-broken throng.

"We will die with him," they cried in their zeal and affection.

He was led away by guards and soldiers to a level plain near the city, and there, surrounded by his faithful followers, Cyprian, Bishop of Carthage and leader of all the Christians in North Africa, suffered martyrdom.

Not only men but women too were persecuted for their faith in these early days of Christianity. The beautiful legend of St Cecilia, the musician, is one of the earliest handed down to us through the long ages. She was a noble Roman lady, who suffered martyrdom when Constantine was quite a little boy. Her parents, who secretly professed Christianity, brought her up in their own faith, and from her earliest childhood she was remarkable for her enthusiasm over it.

Night and day she carried a copy of the Gospel concealed among the folds of her robe. She loved music, and composed hymns which she sang to herself so sweetly that, says the old legend, angels descended from heaven to listen to her. She invented the organ, and she is usually represented in the old pictures with reeds of organ pipes in her hands. When she was sixteen her parents married her to a rich young pagan Roman, to whom she soon taught her own Christian faith. He was afterwards thrown into a dungeon and put to death for his belief.

At last Cecilia was sent for and ordered to sacrifice to the gods. Tall, young, and beautiful, she smiled scornfully at the idea, while those around her wept and entreated her to yield. So firm was her refusal that others became Christians on the spot, and declared themselves ready to die with her.

St Cecilia before her judge.

"What art thou, woman?" cried the judge, struck with terror.

"I am a Roman of noble race," she answered.

"I ask of thy religion," he said.

"Thou blind one, thou art already answered," she replied.

Enraged at her cool determination, the judge ordered that she should be put to death, but the hand of the executioner trembled so that he could not kill her. He wounded her and went away. For three days she lived, singing to the end.

A beautiful and simple white marble statue of St Cecilia may be seen to-day in the church dedicated to her memory in Rome; while poets have ever since loved to sing of this early Christian martyr, who preferred to die rather than to give up the faith.

CHAPTER 10

A NEW ROME

"Till truer glory replaces all glory,
As the torch grows blind at the dawn of day."
—Mrs Browning.

Over two thousand five hundred years ago a little fleet of galleys toiled painfully against the current up the long strait of the Hellespont, rowed across the Sea of Marmora, and anchored in the smooth waters of the first inlet which cuts into the European shore of the Bosphorus. Here a long crescent-shaped creek, which after ages were to call the Golden Horn, strikes inland for seven miles, forming a quiet backwater from the rapid stream running outside. On this headland a few colonists landed, and dragged their ships up on the beach.

These colonists were Greeks, and their colony, known as Byzantium, is now our Constantinople. The Black Sea, which washes its shores, had ever been regarded as a region of fable and mystery. Here was the realm of the Golden Fleece; here the old Argonauts had encountered the fierce north wind which had made them give this part the name of Inhospitable, until a later race renamed it Hospitable from its friendly port. It was in the same spirit that the seamen who ventured south, two thousand years later, turned the name of the "Cape of Storms" into that of the "Cape of Good Hope."

From the very first this colony of Byzantium was a success. One of the strongest fortresses in the Eastern world, it was here that the emperor of the East made his last stand against his brother-in-law Constantine, emperor of the West. Here Constantine besieged him till the city surrendered, and the Roman emperor stood a victor on the ramparts which were ever afterwards to bear his name. He knew the old city well, every inch of it; and he now determined to make it into a new Rome, a new capital for the great Empire over which he now ruled supreme—a new centre for Christianity. The limits of the new city were at once marked out. The emperor, says an old story, marched on foot, followed by all his court, and traced with his spear the line where the new forts were to be built. As he paced farther and farther westward along the shore of the Golden Horn, more than two miles from the old gates, his attendants grew more and more surprised at the vastness of his scheme. At last they spoke, and reminded him that the city was already large enough. But Constantine turned to rebuke them.

"I shall go on," he said, "until he, the Invisible Guide who marches before me, thinks fit to stop."

It was perhaps natural that Constantine should wish the new city to be built as much as possible on the lines of the old capital away on the river Tiber. It must have a forum, a circus, and baths. It was said that every rich city in the world was stripped bare to adorn the new capital, but all the efforts of Constantine failed to make of Constantinople a second Rome. The golden milestone marking the central point of the world was here; here was the Imperial palace; a lighthouse lit up ships in the Bosphorus at night,—all was as complete as human hands could make it.

There is an old story which tells how Constantine managed to attract some of the rich and powerful Romans to live in the new city. When he began to build, he sent twelve rich Romans on an embassy to Persia. At the end of sixteen months they returned to report to the emperor. He invited them to dine with him in his new capital. In the course of conversation he asked them when they intended returning to their palaces and families in Rome.

"Not for some weeks," they replied.

"You will find yourselves there this evening," said the Emperor.

Dinner over, each was conducted by an imperial servant to a palace built exactly like his own in Rome, and on entering each found his room filled with his own furniture, while his wife and family came forward to welcome him home.

46

The city was dedicated on May 11th, 330, celebrated after the Roman fashion by a great festival, with games which lasted forty days.

Seven years later Constantine the Great died in his capital.

His work was done. He had lived to see the heathen empire of Rome changed to the Christian empire of Constantinople through his own energy and power; he had changed the very seat of the world's government; he had made Christianity the state religion, and stopped the persecutions which had tarnished the reigns of his forerunners.

For the proud city on the river Tiber the sun was already setting. High had been the glory of her noon-day, dark was the shadow of her night.

"She sees, she hears, with soul unstirred,
And lifts no hand and speaks no word."

CHAPTER 11

THE ARMIES OF THE NORTH

"See ye the banners blazoned to the day,
  Inwrought with emblems of barbaric pride?"
                        —SHELLEY.

ROME was dying. But by her death other nations were to spring into existence and accomplish their part in the great history of the world. Outside the bounds of the world-empire were many countries still plunged in a shadow-land such as Greece and Rome had once been in the long ago days of which we have learnt.

Away on the far banks of the frozen Danube lived hordes of wild barbarians, known as the Goths. They were tall, fair, strong, and brave men. Living on the borders of the Roman Empire, too, they had learnt Roman ways. Some of their young men fought in the Roman army, some had become Christians; and a Gothic translation of the Gospels may still be seen in Sweden, their early home, written on purple vellum in silver letters.

But some thirteen years after the death of Constantine a great change took place in the position of the Goths.

Suddenly a horde of squalid savages appeared from the wild regions of Central Asia: each man was short and fierce looking, each rode a pony as ugly and unkempt as himself. They were the terrible Huns, who had fought their way over the high tablelands of Asia till they reached the Sea of Azov and found the land of the Goths. On rolled the flood of invaders, striking terror before them, conquering the lands of the Goths, pressing ever on and on toward the Danube, the great Roman boundary.

Dreading the fate that awaited them, the Goths looked across the broad Danube with its well-tilled plains beyond; and at last they crossed over. Day after day and night after night ships crossed and recrossed the Danube, till thousands of Gothic warriors with their wives and children stood on the soil of the Roman Empire, while the watchfires of the Huns blazed away behind them on the other side of the river.

They had made a compact with the Romans before they had taken the important move; but very soon that compact was broken, and a few years' time found the Goths and Romans at war.

Under their young king Alaric they prepared for battle, determined to cut themselves loose from the old and decaying empire, and to hew out new realms for themselves with their own trusty broadswords. A striking army they must have made, with their tall strong figures, their long curling hair and beards, their short girdled tunics with wide turn-down collars and short sleeves, the long trousers which contrasted strangely with the bare-legged Romans.

Leaving Constantinople on their left, the Goths overran the open country of Macedonia. There was no Alexander the Great to oppose them. They passed through the narrow defile of Thermopylæ, but there was no Leonidas and his Spartan Three Hundred to hold the pass against them. All over the sacred places of Grecian story—Corinth, Argos, Sparta—the tall barbarians swarmed. Athens alone escaped, because, says an old story, Alaric saw the goddess Athene going round about the towers of the Acropolis and Achilles the hero wrathfully guarding the walls.

His thoughts now turned westward. Constantinople was matchless in its strength, Rome was pitiable in her weakness.

"Alaric, delay not; thou shalt penetrate to the city," said an unknown voice ever in his ear.

In the year 400 he obeyed the mysterious summons and entered Italy. Slowly he crossed the snowy Alps, the women and children in Gothic waggons, the warriors on their war-horses, Alaric himself probably full of schemes for the future when he had "penetrated to the city."

But this time he was driven back, and he had to wait ten years before he could accomplish his cherished ideal.

His next march over the north of Italy was like a triumphal procession. He plundered city after city, till at last he came to the walls of Rome. He had already cut off the food-supply of the city by possessing himself of the Port of Rome, so that the great ships from Alexandria could no longer supply grain for the capital. He then waited till hunger and pestilence drove the senators to sue for peace. They begged for honourable terms, for they would rather die than yield.

"The thicker the grass, the easier it is to mow," was Alaric's heartless answer.

He must receive all the gold and silver within the walls, and all the foreign slaves, before he granted peace.

"What do you leave us then?" the senators asked.

"Your lives," replied the barbarian conqueror.

It was the 24th of August 410, when at last Alaric and his Gothic army passed through the gates of Rome. It was over eight hundred years since the wild Gauls had slain the old fathers in the Forum, eight hundred years since a foreign foe had set foot in the "Eternal City."

Terrible were the sufferings of the Romans during the six days that the Goths pillaged their once famous city. The news was carried to the feeble-minded emperor, who had long ago escaped from Rome and was keeping poultry in the country.

He had called his hens by names, and one was known as "Rome."

"Rome has perished," cried the messenger, hastening into the presence of the young emperor.

"That cannot be, for I have just fed her out of my hand," cried the distressed poultry-keeper.

Then the messenger explained that it was the city and not the hen, which seemed almost a relief to the emperor, as he murmured, "But I thought, my friend, that my bird 'Rome' had perished."

Such was the capture of Rome by barbarian hordes. By her fall other nations were to rise, for the civilisation she had taught was to spread through these very barbarians even to the ends of Europe.

CHAPTER 12

THE DARK AGES

"The old order changeth, yielding place to new."
—TENNYSON.

THE next few hundred years are known to history as the Dark Ages. It seemed as if the world were falling into chaos. The Western Empire had fallen, the Eastern stood on no too sure foundation. Europe had lost her guide and her rudder: the central power was gone.

No firm decrees now went forth from the Roman emperor, for Roman emperor there was none. No legions bearing the Roman Eagle guarded the boundaries of the Rhine and the Danube, for boundary there was none. The last Roman, standing at the stern of his departing vessel, had waved his sad "Farewell, Britain," on his recall to protect the capital against the Goths. The strong arms of Rome were powerless.

And over all her lost country surged the savage hordes of barbarians, fighting their way ever westwards and southwards, settling here, invading there, now driving a weaker tribe before them as the

Huns had driven the Goths, now even sailing across the sea to attack some new territory on the outskirts of the empire.

"The barbarians chase us into the sea," groaned the Britons helplessly; "the sea throws us back upon the barbarians, and we have only the hard choice left us of perishing by the sword or the waves."

This was but the expression of many whom the fall of Rome had exposed to the attack of these wild marauders.

These barbarians appeared under various names. There was a powerful tribe, under the name of Vandals, who had already overrun Gaul and crossed the Pyrenees into Spain. From thence they crossed the Mediterranean into Africa. They ravaged the fair coast washed by that great blue inland sea, devastated town after town, and finally took possession of Carthage—the Carthage of Cyprian—which ranked as the Rome of the African world. It was now conquered by the Vandals, and with it the conquest of North Africa was complete.

"Whither shall we sail now?" asked the pilot on board the Vandal ship that was bearing the chief away from Carthage.

"Sail against those with whom God is angry," was the fierce answer.

From time to time during these dark rude ages a savage figure stands out stronger than his fellows to do and dare, a man with more ambition or more determination to conquer and kill.

"For what fortress, what city, can hope to exist if it is our pleasure that it should be erased from the earth?" cried one such man, Attila, in whom the wild Huns had found an able king.

For a time he swept all before him. Passing through Germany to Gaul, he would fain have burst through the barrier of the river Loire, but Theodoric King of the Goths arose and showed himself the equal of Attila the Hun—the Scourge of God, as he was called.

So these wandering nations moved about in search of a home, a fatherland, a city, and a state. All the while they were learning the great lessons that Rome had taught: they were coming into contact with civilised people, and they were becoming civilised themselves. And not only this, but Christian teaching, spreading rapidly now from Constantinople, was playing its part too in the progress of the world's history.

For the moment it seemed as if everything was at a standstill. There were no new schools, the children were untaught. No new highways were forthcoming on land or sea. Everything was dead, lifeless, dreary. "It was as if a torrent of mud had spread over the smiling fields, burying beneath it the fair flowers and rich crops of learning and art so diligently sown by the Greeks."

But a far grander life than Rome could ever have made possible was to spread over the whole of

Europe, westward and ever westward, till at length it should reach the yet unknown land beyond the Atlantic. It was with the story of nations as the poet Tennyson tells us it is with the story of man—

> "For all we thought and loved and did
> And hoped and suffered, is but seed
> Of what in them is flower and fruit."

CHAPTER 13

KING ARTHUR AND HIS KNIGHTS

"A glorious company, the flower of men
To serve as model for the mighty world."
—TENNYSON.

THE story of King Arthur belongs to this period, when the barbarians were swarming over the Western world.

When the Romans left Britain to return to their falling capital, the heathen hosts poured over the seas and swept all before them in that fair island with its open tracts of country, its winding rivers, and its sheltering coast, till the inhabitants had to take refuge in the western part known as Wales.

And the Britons groaned for the Roman legions there again and Cæsar's eagle, till Arthur came.

Now so much story and fable hang round this mysterious King Arthur that it is hard to know what is history and what is romance. Perhaps it does not much matter in this case, for we can accept him as the poets have sung of him—as one of the noblest, purest, grandest of men, who will ever serve as a "model for the mighty world."

Let us hear the story as the poet Tennyson tells it, in all its beauty and in all its strength.

One night, as the old Welsh magician Merlin stood on the sea-shore, a wave washed to his feet an infant, who was none other than the future King Arthur.

"From the great deep to the great deep he goes."

Merlin took the babe, who grew to manhood in solitude, until the time came when he should be discovered and crowned King of Britain. But he had to conquer the barbarians, known as Saxons, many times before his people would believe in him.

Then he formed a brave band of knights to help him in his work, to break the heathen and uphold the Christ, to ride abroad redressing human wrongs, to fulfill the boundless purpose of their King. They were known as the Knights of the Round Table, because Arthur, not wishing to honour one above another, had a round table made at which all sat at meals.

It would take too long to tell of all the famous deeds wrought by the king and his knights: how Arthur was ever fighting, his armour shining with gold and jewels, his helmet glistening with a golden dragon at the top, his precious sword Excalibur ever in his right hand.

Again and again he waged war against the heathen tribes as well as against the evils of the times. The story of the Quest for the Holy Grail—a cup supposed to have been used by Christ—is one of the most beautiful in connection with King Arthur.

"Lords and fair knights," said the king one day when sitting at the Round Table, "as ye well know, there is a cup which hath ever been held the holiest treasure of the world. Heaven hath hidden it, none knows where. Yet somewhere in the world it still may be. And may be it is left to this noble order of the Table Round to find and bring it home. Many great quests and perilous adventures have ye all taken, but this high quest he only shall attain who hath clean hands and a pure heart, and valour and hardihood beyond all other men."

The knights set off on the quest for the Holy Grail, but only Sir Galahad—the bright boy-knight—Sir Percival, and one other among the many knights, were good enough and brave enough to see the vision.

This time-worn story has taken such hold upon the minds of men, that to this very day, in the little town of Bayreuth in the heart of Bavaria, the Quest for the Holy Grail is still acted, music and words being composed by Wagner, one of the world's great musicians.

But the day came when Arthur was wounded in that last dim, weird battle of the West, with a death-white mist sleeping over sand and sea—wounded unto death.

> "So all day long the noise of battle rolled
> Among the mountains by the winter sea
> Until King Arthur's Table, man by man,
> Had fallen."

One faithful knight, Sir Bedevere, was left; and finding his king was deeply wounded, he carried him to a little chapel near the battlefield.

It was evening, and the moon was full. Arthur felt he was dying. The men he had loved were sleeping their last sleep on the battlefield; never more should they all delight their souls with talk of knightly deeds. The time had come to part with the jewelled sword Excalibur. The story runs that this sword was the gift of a mysterious Lady of the Lake; that in the old days, one summer noon, an arm rose from out a lake holding the sword, which Arthur rowed across the water and took. Now Excalibur must be thrown back into the lake, and Sir Bedevere must do the deed.

Obedient to the king's commands the knight took the sword, and climbing by zigzag paths came on the lake. The beautiful jewels sparkled in the moonlight, and Bedevere could not make up his mind to throw it away, so he hid it among the reeds and returned to the king. But Arthur soon discovered his deceit and sent him again to do his bidding. Again Sir Bedevere went; again his courage failed; again he returned to the dying king.

"Ah, miserable and unkind, untrue, unknightly, traitor-hearted," cried Arthur; "authority forgets a dying king. Get thee hence, and if thou spare to fling Excalibur I will arise and slay thee with my hands."

Then the knight rose quickly, hastened to the lake, and shutting his eyes flung the good sword into the water. The arm rose up, grasped it firmly, brandished it three times, and drew it down into the water. Then Arthur was content. With the help of Sir Bedevere he managed to get to the lake himself. There a barge was waiting for him.

"I am going a long way," said the dying king to his weeping knight, "to the island valley of Avilion, where falls not hail, or rain, or any snow, nor ever wind blows loudly, but it lies deep-meadowed, happy, fair with orchard lawns, where I will heal me of my grievous wound."

Then the barge, with oar and sail, moved slowly away over the cold moonlit lake, and Sir Bedevere watched it till it was out of sight.

"The king is gone," he moaned at last. "From the great deep to the great deep he goes."

Such is the story the poet tells. It may not be true, but the fact remains that there once lived a king of early Britain who fought against the barbarians known as Saxons, and that though they finally conquered and gave their name to the new country, King Arthur did not live and fight in vain.

CHAPTER 14

THE HERO OF TWO NATIONS

"The greatest man of the Middle Ages."
—DE QUINCEY.

THE England for which Arthur had fought—for which he had died—was now in the hands of his old foes the Saxons; but as the years rolled on it was evident that a nation over the seas was rising to a dangerous greatness. This was the power of another tribe known as the Franks, and the man who led the Franks to victory, who made of them a great nation and so created our modern Europe, was Charles the Great, or Charlemagne, as the poets call him.

As quite a little boy this Charlemagne had accompanied his father, Pepin, from his home in North Germany to Italy to fight there, and for his services Pepin the Short was made king of the Franks. An ardent Christian himself, he spent his life spreading Christianity through his kingdom and checking the wandering heathen tribes. When Charlemagne succeeded him, this too was the object of his life. It seems a strange thing in these days to teach the gospel of peace with the edge of the sword, but Charlemagne thought it the right thing. He soon became a hero in the eyes of his people. He was tall and strong, with the eyes of a lion, a will of iron strength, and an energy that was dauntless.

"The best man on earth and the bravest was Charlemagne," said the Saxons, though they had every cause to hate the rival Franks; for had they not sprung from a common parent, the Germans?

Not only had he the Saxons in the north to fight, but he must needs go south and conquer the Lombards, who were again overrunning Italy, and against whom he had fought with his father when quite a little boy. Once more he was victorious: for his success he was crowned in Rome as King of the Lombards, and so added a large part of North Italy to his already large kingdom.

He was now a marked man, and Spain cried out to him to come and help her against her foes, the Arabs or Moors, who had swept over the land from the East. In the course of the next few years he had conquered all the land down to the sea, and his banners were riddled through. He was returning over the Pyrenees when a sad thing happened. The tragic death of his young nephew Roland has been a favourite subject with poets and singers, until it has become difficult to know what is fact and what is fiction. Here is the story.

The main army under Charlemagne had reached the borders of Spain, leaving Roland in command of the rear-guard, some way behind. Roland led his men up a long rocky pass, and they had climbed a mountain ridge, when, looking down, they saw the valley below bristling with spears, while the murmur of this mighty pagan host rose to them on the mountain top as the murmur of the sea.

"What shall we do?" asked his trusted friend and companion.

"This will we do," answered Roland calmly. "When we have rested we will go forward, for sweet it is to do our duty for our king."

"But," said his friend, "we are but a handful, and these are more in number than the sands of the sea. Be wise. Take your horn, good comrade, and sound it; perchance Charlemagne may hear, and come back with his host to succour us."

"God forbid I should sound my horn and bring the king back, and lose my good name and bring disgrace upon us all," answered Roland proudly.

There was not a man but loved Roland unto death, and cheerfully they obeyed him. So the little band of men charged down the mountainside into the valley of death, ever following their leader and the snow-white banner carried by the guard. For hours they fought that great pagan host, till at last hardly a handful of Franks were left.

"Blow thy horn, blow thy horn," urged his friends. And Roland put the horn to his mouth and blew a great blast. Far away up the valley went the sound, and it reached the ears of Charlemagne.

"Listen, what is that?" he cried; "surely our men do fight to-day."

"It is only the sighing of the wind," said the traitor who was with him.

Weary with battle, Roland took his horn again and winded it with all his strength. So long and mighty was the blast that the veins stood out upon his forehead in great cords.

"Hark, it is Roland's horn," cried Charlemagne again, and again they persuaded him that Roland was but hunting in the woods.

Then in sore pain and heaviness Roland lifted the horn feebly to his lips and blew for the last time. Charlemagne now started up; the salt tears gathered in his eyes and dropped upon his snowy beard.

"Oh Roland, my brave captain, too long have I delayed," he sobbed; and with all his host he set out at full speed for Roland.

Meanwhile Roland fought on—fought till every man of the rear-guard lay dead and he himself was sore wounded. When he found that he was dying, he lay down and set his face towards Spain and towards his enemies, that men should see he died a conqueror. By him he put his sword and his horn. "They will see that the guard has done its duty," he said to himself contentedly. Then, raising his weary hands to Heaven, he died.

The low red sun was setting in the west when Charlemagne and his host rode up, and there was not a man in all that host that did not weep for pity at the sight before them now.

But Charlemagne had fallen on his face on Roland's dead body, with an exceeding bitter cry, for the knight was passing dear to him.

Right gladly would he have given Spain and all the fruits of that war to have had Roland back again. But Charlemagne had work to do in his own great realm. He dreamt of uniting all the conquered countries—all the heathen tribes that had so long been at war with each other—into one great empire, in which the power and learning of ancient Rome should be united to a Christian religion.

Was this dream realised when, in the year 800, he was made Emperor of Rome? It was Christmas Day, and Charlemagne was kneeling with his two sons in the church of St Peter, when suddenly a crown of gold was placed on his head, while voices thundered forth the old formula: "To Charles the Augustus, crowned of God, the great and pacific Emperor, long life and victory." Thus the Roman Empire of the West, which had fallen more than three hundred years before, was now restored by Charlemagne the Frank.

CHAPTER 15

THE HARDY NORTHMEN

"The sea is their school of war, and the storm their friend."

THE great Charlemagne was still ruling wisely and well over his mighty province, when a trouble arose on the coasts destined to have far-reaching results.

Away in the far north of the country we now call Norway, Sweden, and Denmark lived a hardy rugged race known as the Northmen or Danes. They were closely connected with the Angles and Saxons who had set sail for Britain years before and overrun it in the days of King Arthur. Like the Greeks of old, these people had passed through an age of legend. They had worshipped their god Odin or Woden, from whom we get the day of the week called Wednesday; the god Thor, from whom we get Thursday; and the god Frigga, from whom we get Friday.

In appearance these Northmen were broad, deep-chested, tall men, with the fair hair and blue eyes of the Saxons. Dressed in long stockings, high shoes, shirts, loose drawers, and low hats, they carried in times of war long shields, axes, spears, and swords.

But the sea was the home of these people—Vikings, as they were often called, from the word *vic*, meaning a bay or fiord. The stern climate and barren soil of their inhospitable northern home drove them forth over the stormy waters to get a livelihood by pillage and plunder. Their black ships, standing high above the water, prow and stern ending in the head and tail of some strange animal, struck terror into the hearts of all who saw them, as they swept over the stormy seas in search of plunder and pillage.

So much did they trouble Charlemagne that an old story tells us how he took the young children of the Northmen and slew all those who were taller than his sword. Another story says he was sitting one day in his palace near the sea-side, when from his window he saw the flash of Viking sails far out at sea.

"These are no merchants," he cried, rising from his seat.

He watched till the ships were out of sight, then shedding bitter tears, he added: "I am very sorrowful, for I see what woes these men will bring on my subjects."

Charlemagne was right: they were to become a terror to all, and to play a large part in the history of the world. Little did he dream that they would conquer a large part of his kingdom, to be called, after themselves, Normandy. Little did Alfred the Great, King of England, dream that these very

Charlemagne saw the Viking sails.

Northmen should one day sweep over his country, and that from these Vikings of olden times the English race should spring. Not since the Phœnicians had there been such a sea-going race of men, fearless and free, with a spirit of daring and a love of adventure that neither Greeks nor Romans had ever possessed.

Wondrous are the stories of these old Viking heroes, who would set forth with a few followers to discover new lands, fight strange people, and return home with rich plunder to their bleak north country. They soon sailed over to the islands of Orkney and Shetland at the north of Scotland, and away beyond to Iceland, and beyond that again to Greenland.

After the death of Charlemagne in 814 the Northmen became bolder. They sailed up the large rivers, and actually laid siege to Paris. One of their leaders was called Rollo, and many are the stories told of this famous old Viking. So stout was he that no horse could carry him, and he had to walk everywhere. When quite young he left his home and sailed about the seas, leading the life of a pirate.

The King of Norway wished to stop these sea rovers and robbers, and made strict laws against them. Rollo broke all these, and he was exiled for life from his native land. He collected a band of wild young men like himself, and sailed away from the home he was never to see again. The company of adventurers landed in France, and the king went forth with his army to meet them.

"Why have you come to France?" he asked them.

"To conquer it," was the stout reply.

"Would you not rather do homage to the king?" was the next question.

"No," shouted the whole band as one man.

So a battle was fought, in which the French were beaten, and the Vikings marched victoriously to Rouen, where Rollo was chosen to be chief.

After a time Rollo planned an expedition into the heart of France, and the king was so much alarmed that he offered to give Rollo that northern part of France called Normandy—the land of the Northmen. And from this time a change came over the wild Viking. He divided the new land among his followers, in return for which they were to follow him to battle when he summoned them. He became a Christian and a good ruler. He adopted the language of the country, and after a time there was no need for the terror-stricken people of the north to sob out their despairing petition—

"From the fury of the Northmen, save us, Lord."

CHAPTER 16

HOW THE NORTHMEN CONQUERED ENGLAND

"Of one self-stock at first
Make them again one people—Norman, English;
And English, Norman."
—TENNYSON (Harold).

THE Northmen had been settled in Normandy more than a hundred years, and one William—afterwards known to history as William the Conqueror—was ruling over the country. He had ruled since he was a little boy of seven years old, his father having died on a pilgrimage to the Holy Land. The wise men of Normandy had objected to the appointment of one so young as their duke.

"He is little, but he will grow," said his father, as he bade them farewell.

The young Norman duke soon showed himself to be above his fellows. The spirit of the old Vikings seemed to be in him. He was a young giant in size, in strength, and in courage. His whole life was spent in mastering difficulties.

"No knight under heaven," confessed his enemies, "was William's peer."

Man and horse went down before his lance: no man could bend his bow. Pitiless as he was strong, he could refuse a grave to his fearless foe, Harold of England, at the close of his greatest victory. He cared not whether men hated or loved him. They neither loved him nor did they hate him. They feared him.

Now this William had made a friend of the King of England, whose name was Edward the Confessor. The young Norman duke had been over to visit England, and the King of England had been in Normandy, and had taken back a large number of Normans to England with him, which was bitterly resented by his Saxon subjects.

There was a Saxon earl called Harold, who was a very powerful man in England at this time. Very beautiful, too, was this Harold. He had long fair hair reaching to his shoulders in one thick curl, he had deep blue eyes which flashed brightly, and a smile that had already won the hearts of the English people. He too had been to Normandy, and knew well William, the Norman Duke. Indeed it had already dawned in the minds of both these men that they were rivals for the throne of England when the present king, Edward the Confessor, should die.

The day came, and Edward died in the arms of Harold the Saxon, who was at once proclaimed King of England amid the shouts of the people: "We choose thee, Harold, for our lord and king."

The Norman duke was in the forest at home trying some new arrows with some of his Norman knights. Suddenly a rider came at full speed, and drawing William aside, whispered hastily, "King Edward is dead, and Harold is king of all England!"

"Edward dead? Then England is mine," cried William.

But England was not his yet. Huge difficulties stood in his way, but he was accustomed to difficulties. He had no fleet, no ships to cross the Channel. His Norman knights too objected. They said he was rash, that it was not their duty to follow him over the seas to England.

But William's firm resolve won the day. Trees were cut down and ships were built. All through the long summer days the havens of Normandy were busy, building and manning their ships, until by August some six hundred were ready. Then they waited a whole month on the French coast for a south wind to blow them over to England. At last a south wind arose, and the fleet set sail in the night, the duke's own ship sailing first, with a huge lantern at the masthead to guide them. They landed near Pevensey, on the south coast of England, some twelve miles from Hastings, near which the great battle was so soon to be fought. An old story says as William stepped on English ground his foot slipped, and he fell. Rising with his hands full of earth, "I have taken possession of my kingdom," he said, "for the earth of England is in my hands."

When Harold the Saxon heard that William of Normandy was preparing to fight him for the English throne, he hurried south with his army. It was the 14th of October 1066 when the two armies met near Hastings for the final struggle. The night before the battle which was to decide the fate of England was spent by the Saxons over their fires, singing merrily, eating and drinking; spent by the Normans in prayer.

When morning dawned Harold and his army were found to be on the hill above Hastings, ready for the Norman attack. His bodyguard—men in full armour with huge axes—were grouped round the standard of the king. The rest of his army was composed of half-armed rustics, who, loving him, had flocked to his summons to fight with the stranger. Against these were arrayed the knighthood of Normandy. In front rode a minstrel, tossing his sword in the air and catching it again, as he chanted the song of Roland. All the fury of fight that glowed in his Norseman's blood spurred William the Conqueror onwards up the slopes with his men. Again and again they were driven back. Then a cry rang out that he was slain.

"I live," he cried, tearing off his helmet, "and, by God's help, I will conquer yet."

And he did. All day long the battle raged. The Normans were gaining the hill now. By six o'clock they had reached the standard and Harold's bodyguard. Suddenly William ordered his archers to shoot their arrows up in the air. As Harold raised his eyes an arrow struck one, and he fell.

"Fight on: conceal my death," he gasped.

Then, struggling to his feet, he tried to raise his battle-axe to deal another blow for his beloved country, but in vain. His strength was spent.

> "Every man about his king
> Fell where he stood."

The battle was over. William the Norman had conquered England. Harold, the last of the Saxon kings, was dead. They laid him beneath a heap of stones on the "waste sea-shore."

"For," said William, "he kept the shore while he lived; let him guard it now he is dead."

So William the Conqueror was crowned King of England, and the Northmen entered at last into possession of the island they had long coveted.

CHAPTER 17

A SPANISH HERO

"Hadst thou lived in days of old,
O what wonders had been told."
—KEATS.

WHILE the Vikings were sailing over the stormy seas in their great black ships, and while the Normans were crossing over to England to complete their conquests, the Moors from the far East were again overrunning Spain.

These Moors or Arabs were not pagans like the Northmen, the Goths, the Vandals, or the Saxons: they called themselves Mohammedans, or followers of the prophet Mohammed.

Mohammed was born in the sixth century after Christ, about the time when King Arthur was ruling over Britain. But not till he was forty years old did Mohammed come forth and assume the title of prophet.

One day, says an old story, he was wandering in the solitary desert-land around Mecca, depressed and melancholy, when he heard a voice, and beheld

78

between heaven and earth an angel, who assured him that he—Mohammed—was the prophet of God. Nothing doubting, the new prophet came forth and began to teach this: That there was One God, and that Mohammed was his prophet.

To the ignorant wandering Arabs this was a new light. They flocked round Mohammed. His commanding presence, his keen black eyes, his flowing beard, his gracious smile and eloquent teaching, drew more and ever more to his side. His followers increased rapidly. He could not write, but he dictated his doctrines; and they were written down in a book called the Koran, which is to the Mohammedans to-day what the Bible is to the Christians. Mohammedanism is still the religion used chiefly in the East.

"Who goes there?" cries the watchman nightly in the streets of Cairo; and the dusky Arab passes with the answer, "There is no God but God."

These Arabs, then, who had roamed unnoticed in their desert-lands since the very earliest times, now sprang into fame. United in one faith, their armies making converts as they went, they conquered North Africa, and finally became masters of Spain. Charlemagne and Roland had fought against them, but now they were rulers over a great part of the country.

It was at this time that the Cid—the great popular hero of Spain—arose to deliver his country from the power of the Arabs, to deliver Christians from the influence of Mohammedanism.

The story of the Cid is mixed with legend and fable; but there is much truth lying under the husks of legend, and many a sound kernel of history wrapped up in the old fables. And to tell the story of Spain without the story of the Cid would be like telling the story of old Greece without the story of Achilles.

Roderick Diaz is the glory of Spain, the hero of the people, the perfect warrior, the ideal man-at-arms; and he lives in the heart of the nation as does Arthur in England or Roland in France.

The Cid, from a word meaning Lord, was born in 1026, and soon rose to fame. When yet a stripling, not twenty summers old, he led an army of Christian warriors against the Arabs, who had entered a province called Castile in the north of Spain. Five kings led the Arab army, but the Cid defeated them among the Spanish mountains and drove them back.

Not only was their beloved Cid brave in battle and merciful in peace, sang the old poets, but he was kind to those in trouble. Here is a story they tell. After his victory over the five Moorish kings he set out on a journey with his knights and followers. As they journeyed they found a poor leper, stuck fast in the mud, shouting for help. The Spanish knights passed by, but the Cid leaped from his horse, lifted the poor man to his saddle, and took him back. At table that night he shared his plate with the afflicted man, and took him to his own bed. At midnight he awoke. The leper was gone, but he saw a form clothed in dazzling white.

"I, whom thou didst take for a poor leper and didst help—I am St Lazarus," said a voice. "And in return for what thou hast done for the love of God, thou mayst ask whatever thou wilt and it shall be accomplished. Thou shalt be feared by Moor and Christian, and never shall thy enemies prevail over thee."

Faithfully, indeed, did the Cid serve his king; but after a while there were men who whispered evil against him, and the king was angry with the Cid and bade him leave Spain within nine days, never to return. Sadly the Cid went forth from his own city, while men and women wept at the thought of their hero leaving them for ever. But the king forgave him after a time, and the Cid came home again and helped his country against the Moors. He besieged Valencia, which was one of the richest towns in the kingdom, and took it after a desperate resistance from within.

The Cid ruled the city for some years both wisely and well. But again a great Moorish host came against the city led by a king from North Africa. The Cid had grown old and feeble, and his long beard was snowy white, and he knew that death was near. Yet he had been told in a vision that he should still conquer the Moors. The Cid called his people around him: then he spoke. He was very weak, but his voice was clear.

"Ye know that the king will soon be here with seven-and-thirty other kings and with a mighty power of Moors," he said. "After I have departed see that ye utter no cries, that the Moors may not know of my death, but sound your trumpets and tambours and make the greatest rejoicings you can. Then saddle ye my horse and arm him well, and ye shall apparel my body full seemly, and place me upon the horse, and fasten and tie me thereon so that I cannot fall."

The next day the Cid died. And they dressed his body and set it on his beloved horse, supported by a framework of boards. They hung his shield about his neck, they placed his sword upright in his hand, and they led their dead hero against his foes.

The Moors came on. "But it seemed to them that there came against them on the part of the Christians full seventy thousand knights, all as white as snow, and before them a knight of great stature upon a white horse with a cross of blood, who bore in one hand a white banner, and in the other a sword which seemed to be of fire." The Moors were so terrified that they fled, never stopping till they reached the sea. And so great was the press that numbers were drowned before ever they could reach the ships.

So the Cid conquered the Moors even in death, according to this old story; but after all it is but a story of the old days in Spain.

CHAPTER 18

THE FIRST CRUSADE

"The true old times,
When every morning brought a noble chance,
And every chance brought out a noble knight."
—TENNYSON.

WHILE the Cid was fighting against the followers of Mohammed in Spain, another people had conquered them in Asia. These were known as the Turks, a savage race who had risen to great power, run over the Holy Land, and taken Jerusalem for themselves. For many years pilgrims had flocked to Jerusalem from all parts of Europe. The Turks now treated them with great cruelty. The complaints spread over Europe, till the Christians of every land were stirred with wrath against the cruel Turk.

About the year 1092 a Frenchman, Peter the Hermit, went on a pilgrimage to Jerusalem. There his soul was stirred by the horrors he saw, the inhuman treatment of the Christian pilgrims, and the want of care towards the holy places. An old story says that he spent the night at the Holy Tomb. Weary with watching, he fell asleep; and as he slept Christ appeared to him in his dreams, bidding him hasten home to make known the woes of the Christians. At dawn he rose, hurried to the coast, and took a ship for Italy to tell the Pope all he had seen and heard.

Urban listened with enthusiasm and eagerly bestowed his blessing on Peter the Hermit, who went forth from his presence to carry the message through the length and breadth of the land. Riding upon an ass, with bare head and feet, carrying in his hand a huge cross, Peter the Hermit went far and wide stirring up the people to go and fight for their brethren in Jerusalem. Rich and poor, old and young, knight and peasant, flocked to hear him.

Then a great meeting was held in France. From a lofty scaffold Pope Urban addressed the crowds, princes and soldiers of France, before him. He urged all of them to go a great expedition to the Holy Land. Dangers would beset their way, sufferings would be their lot, but their reward would be for ever.

"Go then on your errand of love," he cried, full of zeal and enthusiasm. "They who die will enter the mansions of heaven, while the living shall behold the sepulchre of their Lord."

Suddenly a great cry broke from the assembled crowds. "It is the will of God! it is the will of God!" they shouted passionately.

"It is in truth His will," answered the Pope, "and let these words be your war-cry when you unsheath your swords against the enemy. You are

84

soldiers of the cross: wear it as a token that His help will never fail you, as the pledge of a vow which can never be recalled."

Each Crusader fell on his knees.

Men fell on their knees and took vows of service in the Holy War. A red cross marked on the right shoulder was the common sign of all the soldiers thus sworn, and henceforth they were known as Crusaders.

The departure of the great army was fixed for the 15th of August 1096. But before this date a rabble of enthusiasts set out, under Peter the Hermit and Walter the Penniless, for the Holy Land. As might be expected, ignorant of the way, they fell into the hands of fierce tribes who killed them by hundreds, and only Peter the Hermit returned to tell the sad story of their fate.

But the hero of the First Crusade, the model crusader, the perfect knight, was Godfrey de Bouillon. His high birth, fine character, and military courage brought men flocking to his standard, and his great army of Christian enthusiasts started off for their march through Germany and Hungary to Constantinople.

It was Christmas time before the crusaders stood outside the walls of Constantine's capital. Two months later they were across the Bosphorus and standing on the soil of Asia in the eastern world. It was a host vaster than that of Xerxes, mightier than the army of Alexander when he attempted to conquer Asia, that now marched over the site of old Troy. October found them before Antioch, but it was nine months before they succeeded in wresting the city from the Turks, and ten more before they started on their last great march to the Holy City.

The Italian poet Tasso has given us a most wonderful account of the arrival of the crusaders before Jerusalem. He tells us of their joy, mingled as it was with fear and trembling, when their eyes beheld in the distance that town "where Christ was bought and sold,"—how, forgetting all their pains and perils, they each pointed out to one another the longed-for goal. Jerusalem lay in the morning sunshine. Each crusader fell on his knees filled with reverence as he beheld the scene of his desire, and his eyes filled with tears. Putting aside their armour, the crusaders advanced in pilgrim's garb and with bare feet toward the Holy City.

But there was stiff work to be done before Jerusalem was theirs. More than a month passed, until it seemed as if after all the Turks would be victorious. One day, says an old story, in the midst of that deadly struggle a knight was seen on the Mount of Olives, waving his shining shield to rouse the champions of the cross to their supreme effort.

"It is St George the Martyr, who has come to help us," cried Godfrey.

As he spoke all started up. That day they carried all before them, and the first victorious champion of the cross stood on the walls of Jerusalem. The story of the massacre carried out by these Christian knights is not pleasant reading. The horses of the crusaders riding to the temple were up to their knees in blood, says the old chronicle, while the knights showed no mercy to the vanquished.

Barefooted, bareheaded, and clad in a robe of pure white linen, Godfrey knelt at the Holy Tomb. The first great Crusade had been accomplished. The leaders of the army now held a council to decide who should be given the crown of Jerusalem. The choice fell on Godfrey de Bouillon. To the surprise of all, he declined.

"I will not wear a golden crown," he answered, "in a city where my King has been crowned only with thorns."

Still he consented to remain and watch over the Holy Tomb, and with his faithful knight Tancred he bade farewell to the crusaders who now started for home.

So ended the First Crusade—one of the most wonderful expeditions in the history of the world.

CHAPTER 19

FREDERICK BARBAROSSA

"When the hand
Of Barbarossa grasped imperial sway,
That name ne'er uttered without tears in Milan."
—DANTE.

ALTHOUGH Godfrey de Bouillon died within the year, yet for the next half century the Christians kept Jerusalem from the attacks of the Mohammedans around them, till a time came of danger, and strong help was needed from Europe, and the Second Crusade was formed. It was led by the ruler of Germany and the King of France, for by this time the old kingdom of the Franks had disappeared, and our modern countries of Germany, France, and Italy existed separately.

Marching under the banner of the cross in this ill-fated crusade was young Frederick Barbarossa—as he was afterwards called, by reason of his red beard. Though the Crusade itself was a miserable failure, Barbarossa won golden opinions, and when his uncle died he became ruler of Germany.

Charlemagne had conquered the Lombards in the north of Italy and made their towns subject to Germany, but since his day a spirit of independence had grown up among these people, and for many years the German rulers had left them alone. But Barbarossa meant to assert his right over these northern cities of Italy, and he spent his life trying to suppress them, till he found out his mistake.

Ambitious of restoring the old rights, Barbarossa invaded Lombardy with "the arts of a statesman, the valour of a soldier, and the cruelty of a tyrant." He insisted on being crowned with the iron crown of the Lombards, and afterwards in Rome with the golden crown of the Empire. He left discontent behind him when he returned to Germany, and some years later, followed by a brilliant army of knights and nobles, he re-entered Lombardy. By all the passes of the Alps the German soldiers poured into Italy. Cries of despair arose from the freedom-loving cities when the people beheld this vast army. Milan, one of the chief towns, was besieged and starved into submission.

"Milan shall be a desert," Barbarossa declared, as he took his way back to Germany.

But the brave endurance of the Milanese had roused the other towns in Lombardy to fierce rebellion. They now made a league, known to history as the Lombard League, to preserve that liberty which the emperor sought to destroy. They all agreed to rebuild Milan and to defend one another against Barbarossa should he come again.

He did come again. It was in the year 1176 that the German army met the army of the League at a place called Legnano, some fifteen miles from the new town of Milan.

In the centre of the Milanese soldiers was the sacred car of the city, a ponderous waggon drawn by four white oxen harnessed with red trappings. In the centre of this *corrocio*, as it was called, rose a figure of Christ with outstretched arms, supported on a globe, while above towered a lofty mast from which floated the banner of the Republic. An altar, a chest of medicine, bandages for the wounded, and a band of martial music completed the furniture of this quaint vehicle.

To the flower of the troops, under the name of the Company of Death, was entrusted its defence. Its presence inspired the Milanese with courage and enthusiasm. Its loss meant defeat and disgrace, for it was the very heart of the army. An old legend tells how, at the beginning of this battle, two white doves descended upon the out-stretched figure of Christ, as if in token that the blessing of Heaven was resting on the Italians. A tremendous charge of German cavalry made the Lombards give way, and the Germans pressed forward towards the *corrocio* in the centre of the army.

Nine hundred desperate patriots forming the Company of Death defended the sacred car. Seeing the Germans were gaining ground, fearful for the safety of their treasure, they suddenly knelt down and renewed their vow to God that they would perish for their country. Then, excited to a pitch of unwonted zeal, they charged the Germans. The attack was so sudden and so furious that the tide of victory turned.

Encouraged by such an example, the rest of the Italians rushed forward, and the Germans fled, defeated.

Barbarossa was now convinced of the power of the League, and made peace with the Lombards. His defeat proved of value to him, for it changed his stern attitude towards these people to one of mercy, and he turned the restless enemies of Lombardy into contented subjects.

This victorious struggle of the Lombards against Frederick Barbarossa is one of the landmarks of history, for it is the first entry of the people upon the stage of Europe.

Barbarossa was now an old man when he determined to join the Third Crusade, which was starting for Jerusalem. He reached Asia Minor, where he was stopped at a ford by a crowd of pack-horses. Impatient of delay, he, though now nearly seventy years old, set spurs to his horse and plunged into the water. The current was rapid, and the strong charger struggled against it in vain. In the sight of his army the old man was carried away and drowned.

Great was the regret of all. No ruler of Germany ever won a more lasting place in the affections of his people than Barbarossa.

The legends say that he is still sleeping, away among the Salzburg hills, and that his red beard has grown through the granite rock by which he sits. But some day, it says, when the ravens cease to fly round the mountain, he will awake and bring to his old country the dawn of a golden age.

CHAPTER 20

THE THIRD CRUSADE

"For all that they hold holiest, they died that died that day,
And to the Holy Sepulchre their blood hath won a way."
—NEALE.

STORY and romance have crowned the Third Crusade, in which Frederick Barbarossa perished, with a halo of glory. It was less disastrous than the Second, forty years before, but it fell far short of the splendid results of the First Crusade.

Nevertheless the story of the lion-hearted Richard of England, and how he fought Saladin, the famous Mohammedan chief, is always worth hearing, mixed though it be with legend.

Both were brave men. If Richard was not the ideal Christian knight, he was a brave Northman, like his ancestor Rollo, with a warm zeal for the cause of Christ and a thirst for military glory. He threw his whole heart into the expedition, and alike by land and sea he knew better than any other leader how to conduct the war.

Saladin, too, was as brave as a lion. By sheer force of genius he had risen from one of the strong mountain-tribes beyond Arabia to be the greatest Mohammedan ruler of his age. Master of Egypt, Syria, and Arabia, he had included Jerusalem in his conquests. This is what roused Europe to action, and the three leading rulers of Germany, France, and England at once began preparations for marching against this powerful Eastern ruler.

Richard joined his fleet on the coast of Italy, but it was not till the spring of 1191 that he sailed from Sicily for the Holy Land, conquering the island of Cyprus and marrying a wife on the way. He found the crusaders besieging Acre, a town on the coast of Syria. The siege had lasted for two years. In the plain was gathered the crusading host, now suffering greatly from a plague that had broken out in their midst; on the heights of the city were the followers of Mohammed under the black banner of Saladin. Richard, though prostrated with fever, was overwhelmed by remorse for having loitered so long on the road.

A fiery zeal seized him. He was carried on a mattress to conduct operations. Before long Saladin sued for peace, and the banners of France and England floated from the ramparts of Acre.

But the old spirit of the crusaders was gone, and the French king now slipped home to plot against Richard, who soon found that every French and German crusader was banded against him.

The rest of the Crusade was in the hands of Richard now. The Emperor of Germany was dead. The King of France had gone home. He marched southward towards Jerusalem—the object of his goal—but he never reached the Holy City. Discords broke out, disputes took place among the leaders of the army, and, almost within sight of Jerusalem, the crusading army was obliged to turn back.

Richard himself was led to the top of a hill from which he could get a view of the Holy City. But when his guide pointed out the white buildings dimly visible in the distance, the lion-hearted king put his shield before his face, for he could not bear to see the city which he had failed to take from Saladin. So Jerusalem remained in the hands of the Mohammedans in whose hands it is still to-day.

Sadly and sorrowfully Richard sailed away from the Holy Land. As its shores slowly faded from his sight, he stretched out his arms, exclaiming, "Most holy land, may God grant me life to return and deliver thee from the yoke of the infidels."

His name was feared and honoured by the Mohammedans for long after he had gone, and the Arab of Syria would exclaim to his horse when it started or pricked its ears, "Dost think it is King Richard?"

But many an adventure was in store for the English king. His ship was wrecked on the coast near Venice, and he found himself wandering about in Austria, the country of his enemy, one of the leaders of the crusaders with whom he had quarrelled. For a while he wandered from place to place disguised as a pilgrim, but at last he fell into the hands of his enemy and was placed in a castle, strongly guarded, for some months. There is a story told of how, when the people of England were weeping over the disappearance of their king, his faithful minstrel set out to find his master.

One day the minstrel, Blondel, was resting outside the walls of a castle in Austria, wearied with his wanderings, when he heard the notes of an old French song, which Richard used to sing, floating on the air. Eagerly he took up the song, and then listened with beating heart. Again the voice within took up the strain, and Blondel knew he had found his master, Richard of the lion's heart.

So the king returned home on the payment of a large sum of money, but he did not live to lead another Crusade into the Holy Land.

CHAPTER 21

THE DAYS OF CHIVALRY

"My knights are sworn to vows
Of utter hardihood, utter gentleness
And loving, utter faithfulness in love,
And uttermost obedience to the King."
—TENNYSON.

LET us now take a look at Europe during the Crusades, and see how the people of these Middle Ages struggled from out the Dark Ages, which followed the fall of Rome, to something higher and better. We have seen how the Romans had lost their old loyal spirit. Falsehood, treachery, ingratitude—these were among the vices that had crept in to mar their manhood.

A new order of things was coming, which with the rapid spread of Christianity raised the people of Europe to a higher and better state, lifting them then, as now, beyond the civilisations of the East. The Crusades did for the countries of the West that which nothing else had done—they gave unity. A common danger made all men one. A spirit of loyalty and patriotism began slowly to arise. The idea of honourable service dawned on men, and out of the darkness of the past arose a wonderful system of chivalry. The word in French means literally one who rode on horseback; thus the warrior who served on horseback was called a knight. Let us see how a boy could become a knight in these days of long ago, known as the Middle Ages.

Everywhere in Europe had risen great castles in which dwelt the large landowners or lords, the wealthiest men in the kingdoms. To these castles the little boy of seven years old was sent to serve as a page to the great man of the castle. Here he learnt how to use arms, how to ride and to become strong and useful. He learnt to obey, to be courteous, to serve his lords and ladies honourably, and to acquit himself well. At the age of fourteen the page became a squire, and acted as a personal attendant to his lord. If he were brave and true he was soon allowed to accompany his master to the field, to lead his war horse on the march, to buckle on his armour for the fight, keeping ever close to his side to help him in danger and to give him aid in need.

The ambition of every boy was to become a knight himself, a rank which made him equal in dress, in arms, and in title to the rich landowners. If he could distinguish himself in battle, or show himself courteous and honourable in times of peace, he was admitted to this holy order.

The preparation was severe. The young squire was first bathed and arrayed in white robes, in token of the unstained honour required by the laws of chivalry; new armour was given to him, and, sword in hand, he had to watch these arms all night in church till, in the early morning, service was performed. His sword was then laid on the altar and blessed, while some older knight conferred on the young warrior the order of knighthood. As he knelt to take the solemn vow, he swore to protect the distressed, to maintain Right against Might, and never by word or deed to stain his character as a knight and as a Christian.

"Be thou a good and faithful knight," said the older man, touching the kneeling figure before him with the edge of the sword.

Then all present helped to lace on his helmet, gird his sword-belt, and bind on the gilt spurs which were the outward symbols of knighthood.

Added to this, he might now dress in rich silks and wear scarlet, while his horse might be clad in mail.

And still in Europe the different nations have their orders of knighthood, given for some distinguished service to king and country, while each can look back to the ages long past and still boast of a Roland, an Arthur, or a Cid, heroes of the ancient knighthood.

The Crusades, then, were a splendid chance for the young warriors of Europe to win their spurs, to show themselves loyal to their lord and to their king, to maintain Right against Might. So upon the rude manners and customs of the barbarian invaders arose from the Crusades a spirit of chivalry, which added grace and glory to the Middle Ages.

"And the new sun rose, bringing the new year."

CHAPTER 22

QUEEN OF THE ADRIATIC

"Where Venice sate in state throned on her hundred isles."
—BYRON.

ANOTHER result of the Crusades was the great stimulus given to commerce and trade in Europe. Let us take a look at the centre of Europe's trade at this time.

Away in the far north of the Adriatic Sea, which washes the shores of Eastern Italy, are some seventy-two small islands or mud-banks. They are surrounded by the shallow water of the sea, which laps peacefully round their shores—a very network of channels, and pools, and lagoons as they are called. On these islands, and amid this waste of waters, arose Venice, a city famous in the Middle Ages for the genius and industry of her people who had built up for themselves a commercial greatness of which the world was justly proud.

> "There is a glorious city in the sea.
> The sea is in the broad, the narrow streets,
> Ebbing and flowing: and the salt seaweed
> Clings to the marble of her palaces.
> No track of men, no footsteps to and fro
> Lead to her gates. The path lies o'er the sea—
> Invisible."

It seemed an unpromising foundation for such a city; but quantities of salt from the lagoons and unlimited fish from the sea supplied the people with articles of trade, in exchange for which they got timber for their ships among other things. To such a race, life on the water was yet more natural than life on land, and they soon became daring and expert sailors. With each age their ships increased in size and number, until they became the chief carriers of Europe.

The spirit of the Crusades reached this city of the waters, and she sent no less than 207 ships to help Godfrey de Bouillon on the First Crusade. It was to Venice, then, that the future crusaders looked, when they wanted to cross the Mediterranean Sea for the Holy Land. This traffic brought the Venetians into contact with the rich stores of the boundless East, and costly cargoes returned with the returning ships.

This little sea-girt state was ruled over by a duke, or doge, as he was called; and there is a curious old story about one of these doges in the olden days.

Venice had joined the League of Lombardy against Frederick Barbarossa, and had gained a sea victory over the German fleet. In command of the Venetian fleet was the doge. As soon as he touched land on his return from victory, the Pope himself hastened to the shore and presented him with a ring of gold.

"Take this ring," he said, "and with it the sea as your subject. Every year, on the return of this happy day, you and your successors shall make known to all that the right of conquest has made subject the Adriatic to Venice, as a bride to her husband."

The Venetians brought forth their state ship, glorious with new scarlet and gold, its decks and seats inlaid with costly woods and rowed with long banks of burnished oars. Seated on a magnificent throne was the doge. Gliding through the silent canals, now ringing with festal music and the shouts of the triumphant Venetians, this gorgeous ship reached the harbour.

Here the doge dropped the golden ring into the clear still waters of the Adriatic, plighting the troth of Venice in these words: "We wed thee, O Sea, in token of our true and eternal dominion over thee." For six hundred years the Venetians repeated this ceremony, until Venice fell, unable to compete longer with the trade of the New World.

But these were the days of her glory, when as Queen of the Adriatic she ruled the seas of southern Europe. With the start of the Fifth Crusade she showed her full strength. It would take too long to tell how the blind old Doge Dandolo led his countrymen to the wars; of the glorious fleet that sailed so proudly down the Adriatic, with gay streamers, blazoned with the cross, flying in the wind; of the lords and knights of France who sailed from Venice on their way to the Holy Land. But they turned aside from the object of the expedition and sailed to Constantinople instead. When the crusaders beheld the lofty walls and goodly towers of this "Queen of the Earth" there was not a man whose heart did not tremble within him, for "since the creation of the world," says the old chronicler, "never had such an enterprise been attempted by a handful of men."

It was mainly owing to the dauntless ardour of the old doge that Constantinople fell into the hands of the Venetians. Old and blind as he was, he stood upon the prow of his galley, with the standard of St Mark spread before him, urging his people to push on to the shore. Then, the first to leap out, he reassured the fainting hearts of his warriors; and soon the Venetian standard was flying from one of the towers of Constantinople. From the days of Constantine treasure had been collected from all parts of the world and stored in this queen of cities. She had been the seat of learning for centuries, the storehouse and home of all that was beautiful. Now all was swept away: marbles, pictures, statues, prizes from Egypt, Greece, and Rome, which had made Constantine's city the wonder of nations,—all disappeared under the cruel hands of the crusaders.

Dandolo became Doge of Venice and lord of one-eighth of the Roman Empire, and the triumph of Venice was complete.

Still to-day may be seen in Venice the famous bronze horses taken from Constantinople in this thirteenth century by Dandolo, still the streets of water ebb and flow as the silent boats (gondolas) glide from house to house, and still the winged lions of St Mark command this city of the waters, though her ships no longer dominate the sea.

CHAPTER 23

THE STORY OF MARCO POLO

"I cannot rest from travel. I will drink
Life to the lees: all times I have enjoyed
Greatly and suffered greatly."
—TENNYSON.

THE Crusades had brought about a contact of East and West. But though they had raised the general standard of life, and made the riches of the East— gold, silks, spices, and jewels—familiar throughout Europe, yet the geography of the East was strangely misty and undefined. To the men of the Middle Ages the world was still very limited. The great Atlantic, which was soon to open out a new world, was yet known as the Sea of Darkness, and many attempts to fathom its mysteries had ended in dismal failure. Still more alarming was the idea of a Sea of Pitchy Darkness, which was supposed to lie to the East of Asia.

In the north the old Vikings, having discovered Iceland and sailed by the northern shores of America without knowing it, had become a settled people, and no longer terrified the world by their coasting raids. Africa, except for the strip of northern coast and Egypt, was still a closed book, and nothing was known of the south and west.

This was somewhat the state of affairs when Marco Polo arose, travelled away to the far East, sailed on the Sea of Pitchy Darkness, and returned home, after many years, travel-stained and unrecognisable, to give the world an account of his wonderful doings.

It seems somewhat natural to find that Venice was the birthplace of this early explorer, for Venice, as we have seen, had the enterprise of the whole world at this time.

The very year that Marco Polo was born in Venice—1254—his father and uncle had started forth on a trading enterprise to Constantinople. They were away for some fifteen years, and when they came back they had some wonderful stories to tell to the young Marco. They told him how they had reached China and been at the court of the Chinese ruler, the Great Khan, as he was called. The boy was fired with enthusiasm to go to this distant country, and to see for himself the wonders of the mysterious new land.

Two years later, when the father and uncle started off again, they took young Marco with them. They sailed from Venice to Acre; but nothing is related of their journey except that they travelled towards the north-east and north, till, after three and a half years, they reached the city of the Great Khan, who was at his summer home among the hills to the north of Pekin. The great man, "Lord of all the Earth," as he was called, was very glad to see them, and asked at once who was the young man with them.

"Sire," answered his father, " 'tis my son, and your liegeman."

"Welcome is he too," said the Great Khan.

Marco soon picked up the language and customs of the Chinese, and became a great favourite at this strange foreign court. Once the Great Khan sent him on a journey—"a good six months' journey distant." Marco returned safely; and so ably did he state all he had seen and heard that the Great Khan cried, "If this young man live, he will become a person of great worth and ability."

For seventeen years the three Polos stayed in China, and Marco explored countries which to this day are hardly understood. He was the first traveller to cross Asia, describing kingdom after kingdom that he had seen with his own eyes. He was the first to explore the deserts and the flowering plains of Persia, to tell the Western world of China, with its mighty rivers, its multitudes of people, its huge cities and great manufactures. He first told us of Thibet, Burmah, Japan, Siberia, and the frozen ocean beyond. So the years passed on, the Great Khan was growing old, and the Venetians yearned for home; but whenever they hinted at leaving China, the Khan growled refusal.

At last their chance came. A relation of the Great Khan was King of Persia. He had lately lost his wife, and now sent to China for a wife of his own nationality. The Polos were chosen to take her to Persia, because they were hardy and adventurous, and the lady must be sent by sea to Persia.

Fourteen ships were built by the Great Khan, each having four masts and able to carry nine sails, with some two hundred and fifty sailors in each. In these ships the Polos sailed away from China with the bride-elect on board. They took a sorrowful leave of the Great Khan, who gave them numbers of rubies and precious stones. After sailing for three months in the unknown China Sea they came to the island of Java, and after another eighteen months on the high seas they reached Persia, to find that the bridegroom was dead. But his son, the new king, married the lady without more ado, and the Venetians sailed on for home.

So one day, in the year 1295, three men appeared in the streets of Venice. They were dressed in Asiatic clothes and spoke with a foreign accent. It was therefore no great matter of surprise when they were refused admission to the family house of the Polos.

"We have been in the service of the Great Khan in China," they urged, but no one believed them.

So they invited a number of friends to a banquet prepared with great magnificence, and when the hour arrived for sitting down to table, all three came forth clothed in long crimson satin robes, after the fashion of the times. When the guests were seated, they took off these robes and put on others of crimson damask, whilst the first suits were cut up and divided among their servants. Soon after they again changed, this time to crimson velvet, while the damask robes were divided as before.

Dinner over, Marco rose, and fetched the three shabby garments in which they had arrived. With sharp knives they then slit up the seams, and from them took the most priceless jewels—rubies, diamonds, emeralds, and sapphires. So their astonished guests knew they spoke the truth, and all Venice came rushing to do them honour.

They stayed at home for a time, and then Marco Polo was made commander of a great and powerful galley to fight against Venice's rival seaport, Genoa. He was taken prisoner and shut up in Genoa. Here Marco Polo wrote his book of travels, which are interesting reading to-day; and we cannot do better than follow the good advice at the beginning of his book.

"Great Princes, Emperors, and Kings," he says, "and people of all degrees who desire to get knowledge of the various races of mankind and of sundry regions of the world, take this book and cause it to be read to you."

He was an old man when he had finished dictating his travels to his fellow captive, and he returned to Venice to die.

CHAPTER 24

DANTE'S GREAT POEM

"The poet is a heroic figure belonging to all ages."
—CARLYLE.

WHILE Marco Polo was living his curious life in the Chinese Court of the Great Khan, there was growing up in Florence a man who was to become famous for all time. This Italian, Dante, was to be the spokesman of the Middle Ages: he was to be the voice of the last ten silent centuries—a very landmark of history.

Of his life itself there is but little worthy of record. He first makes his appearance at the age of nine—a shy, sensitive boy with large dark dreamy eyes and a curly head full of the strangest fancies.

One day at a children's party in Florence, Dante met the little Beatrice, simply enough dressed in a crimson frock. To the dreamy poet-boy the little girl was the most beautiful thing he had ever seen, and from that day she became, what knighthood was to the young men of the Middle Ages, his ideal, something he must live to be worthy of. Though Beatrice died when Dante was yet a young man of twenty-four, he kept her as his ideal right through his life; and as she plays a large part in his life, so she plays a large part in his great poem.

He was educated after the fashion of his day, but with no printed books his knowledge was necessarily limited. All that he learnt was in Latin, which was the language of all learned people at this time. He served in the wars of his country, for Florence was torn by strife and divided by party; and Dante loved Florence as Socrates had loved Athens. The State accepted his talents and devotion, and by the time he was thirty-five he had risen to a post of honour in the city.

Then disturbances arose, feeling ran high, parties were divided; and the result was that Dante, in the full vigour of his manhood, was exiled from his own city, doomed henceforth to a life of woe and wandering. Not only was he banished from Florence, but if caught he was to be burnt alive. Later it was proposed that Dante should apologise, pay a fine to the State, and return.

"If I cannot return without calling myself guilty, I will never return," answered this man with fixed stern pride.

For Dante now there was no home in the world. He wandered from place to place, from patron to patron, always working to get back to his beloved Florence, but in vain.

"How hard is the path," he exclaims bitterly.

Hard it was indeed. Alone, friendless, hopeless, cast out of his home for ever, to wander over the face of the cold earth, with no living heart to love him, no kindred soul to comfort him, Dante now turned his thoughts to another world, and tried to imagine what it would all be like. And so, brooding over the unknown in speechless gloom, he bursts forth at last into the wonderful song we delight in to this day, known as the Divine Comedy.

It was the story of a vision Dante supposed he saw—a vision of Hell, Purgatory, and Paradise. It took him years to write, for it was written with pain and toil, with "his heart's blood." None could hinder him now, he had found his work to do, he would not rest till that work was done.

"Follow thou thy star," he could say to himself in his extremest need; "thou shalt not fail of a glorious haven."

He has passed from the cold world of reality into the spirit world, and all the Christianity that had been creeping over Europe during the Middle Ages is summed up in Dante's great poem.

But not only is this Divine Comedy of Dante's the first great Christian poem, but it is the opening of a new European era of song, the beginning of a language and a national literature. For it is written in the Italian language, the language of the people, and not in Latin or Greek, the language of the learned only. A few books had been translated into the language of the people by Alfred the Great of England and other scholars, a few songs had been composed in the language of France. But no great work had been written in any of the languages of modern Europe till Dante wrote his great poem in the language of Italy.

So he did more for his country than he can ever have expected to do, when he left it sorrowing and alone, for he laid the foundation of the union of divided Italy. The people in the cities, such as Venice, Milan, and Genoa, were eager to claim Dante as a countryman, one who spoke and wrote in the language of their country. He had become the one world-voice.

The great work done, the poet died, still an exile, it is said, broken-hearted. In the vision of his life he had reached Paradise and had seen again the Beatrice whom he loved, his goal and his ideal.

Here we must leave the poet, but from out the long ages Dante still speaks for those to hear who will:—

"I will be thy guide
And bring thee hence by an eternal place."

CHAPTER 25

THE MAID OF ORLEANS

"The fate of empires and the doom of kings
Lies clearly spread before my childish mind."
—SCHILLER (Maid of Orleans).

ALMOST ever since the death of Dante war had been raging between England and France. For some hundred years it had gone on, until at last it was ended by a young girl known to history as Joan of Arc, the Maid of Orleans. This is a very wonderful story of how the girl, Joan, saved her country and freed it from the hands of the foreigner.

She was born in the year 1412, away in a small village called Domrémy on the outskirts of a great wood. The child loved the forest. Birds and beasts came lovingly to her childish call. She learnt to spin and sew with other little girls, but never to read and write. She was tender to the poor and sick, fond of church and the church bells. But her quiet life was soon broken by the storm of war.

The King of France died and his son was proclaimed Charles VII., but the King of England called himself king and refused to acknowledge the

French ruler. All this reached the ears of Joan, the little maid, dreaming away in her distant home amid the forests. And she "had pity on the fair realm of France."

One summer afternoon, when Joan was about thirteen, she thought she heard a voice saying to her, "Joan, be a good child, go often to church."

After this she often heard voices speaking to her, until one day she heard this: "Joan, you must go to the help of the King of France, for you shall give him back his kingdom."

"But I am only a poor maiden," pleaded Joan; "I know not how to ride to the wars or to lead men-at-arms."

Then she remembered that Merlin, the old magician who had rescued King Arthur, had said that France should be saved by a maiden from the country. Joan wept and prayed, but she knew that somehow she must go and see the king.

"It was for this I was born," she urged, when they laughed at her earnestness.

So at last it was settled that she should be taken to the king. It took eleven days to reach the Court, where Charles was living. Nobles and courtiers awaited the arrival of the peasant girl, half in sport. Even Charles had the playfulness to hide among his courtiers as she entered, but the maid knew him at once. Falling down on her knees before him,—"I am sent you by the King of Heaven to tell you that you shall be crowned King of France," she cried.

The jesting courtiers grew grave, and the young king listened to her earnest pleading. At last Charles consented to let her go and try her fortune against the English, who were besieging the town of Orleans. So Joan of Arc started forth. For her banner, she had worked the lilies of France in gold upon a white ground on one side, while on the other was the face of God looking down from the clouds upon the earth.

As she mounted her charger, clad in white armour from head to foot, her great white banner in one hand, her sword by her side, the rough French soldiers felt proud of following her, for they looked on her as something divine. When she reached Orleans she found her countrymen ready to give up the town, which had been besieged for seven long months by the English. Her appearance brought them hope and fresh courage. At the sight of her, in her shining armour, with her mystic banner raised on high, the English were struck with terror.

"She is a witch," they said among themselves.

Fort after fort had been taken. One strong one remained. Joan was determined to take it. She led out the soldiers against this last fort. The English fought desperately, and the maid fell wounded. She was carried away. Suddenly she heard that the French were failing. Heedless of her wound, she mounted her horse, unfurled her banner, and returned.

"Watch my standard," she cried; "when it touches the walls you shall enter the fort."

The return of this wounded witch at the head of her men filled the English with renewed terror. Suddenly above the din of battle rang out the clear voice of the maid, "The victory is ours!"

It was true. The long weary siege was ended: Orleans belonged to the French once more. And it was all due to the courage and inspiration of Joan of Arc.

Entering the great church at Orleans, she wept so passionately that all the people wept with her. Then, flushed with victory, with the shouts of her fellow-soldiers yet ringing in her ears, she made her way to the king.

"Come and be crowned king at Rheims," she cried, throwing herself at his feet; and two months later she stood in her armour of shining steel, her white banner held on high, to see the king crowned. Her mission was now accomplished and she wished to go home, but the king forced her to remain. The end of the story is very sad. The English declared that she was indeed a witch, and for this she was tried. The trial was a long one, and grossly unfair. Charles put out no hand to save her, though she had won him back his crown and saved his kingdom.

"I hold to my Judge," she cried, as her earthly judges gave sentence against her,—"to the King of heaven and earth."

She was condemned to die. A great pile was raised in the market-place at Rouen, where now her statue stands. Her martyrdom was as heroic as had been her life.

"Oh Rouen! Rouen!" she was heard to murmur, as she looked over the city from her lofty scaffold, "I have great fear lest you suffer for my death. Yes, my voices were from God," she cried suddenly, as the flames curled up around her.

Then her head drooped forward, and with one last cry of "Jesus," the Maid of Orleans perished.

"We are lost," muttered an Englishman as the crowd broke up; "we have burned a saint."

But the French people who loved her tell a story of how, when all was over and the heroic Maid of Orleans was but a heap of smouldering ashes, a beautiful white dove rose up from the smoking pile and flew upward towards the sky. It was the dove Peace, they said, that had spread its wings over the fair land of France, saved by Joan of Arc.

CHAPTER 26

THE SEA OF DARKNESS

"To open up those wastes of tide
No generation opened before."

WE now open a wonderful new chapter in the world's history, a chapter full of mystery, adventure, and discovery, when the spirit of enterprise was awakened and the eyes of all men were turned towards the boundless Sea of Darkness and the unknown lands beyond.

It had been a triumphant day for the old Phœnicians when they had at last sailed through the terrible pillars of Hercules—which were supposed to mark the bounds of the world—and found a great rough sea rolling in beyond the Mediterranean. This farthest point of legendary adventure was now to be the starting point of the new voyagers. Portugal, lying just outside the Pillars of Hercules,—or Gibraltar, as we call the narrow passage now,—was the home of those who were the first to break the charm of the Mediterranean. Until this time the Great Sea had been the centre of all civilisation. Around its shores had been grouped the chief races of mankind—the Phœnicians and Carthaginians, the Greeks and Romans; over her blue waters the traffic of the world had passed.

True, the men of the Middle Ages were beginning to dream of something beyond. Through the dreaded Sea of Darkness had been found narrow belts of light. Ships from Venice braved the dreaded Bay of Biscay to get to the Netherlands for the sake of trading with Bruges and Ghent. It took them eight long months to reach the bleak North Sea from their sunny waters of the Adriatic.

The men of Portugal, the extreme west of Europe, looked out over the rough waters of the Sea of Darkness. Their capital, Lisbon, stood at the mouth of the river Tagus, which flowed into the unknown ocean; and they must often have wondered what lay beyond this great strong sea, the waves of which dashed higher than those of the Mediterranean Sea.

Only five centuries ago this great Atlantic Ocean, across which steamers from all countries are steaming to-day, was described by an old writer as "a vast and boundless ocean, on which ships dare not venture out of sight of land. For even if the sailors knew the direction of the winds, they would not know whither those winds would carry them, and, as there is no inhabited country beyond, they would run great risk of being lost in mist and vapour. The limit of the West is the Atlantic Ocean," adds this old writer with certainty.

But now a great light was to be shed over this mysterious sea. One man—born and bred in Portugal—was to awake his sleeping nation to the wonderful possibilities of the unknown sea. His name was Prince Henry of Portugal. His father was King John of Portugal, and his mother was an Englishwoman—Queen Philippa.

This Queen had shared the throne of Portugal with King John for twenty-eight years, and her son Henry was but twenty when she lay dying. He was just starting with his father and two brothers for a great Moorish port on the African side of the Straits of Gibraltar. The three princes had all asked for knighthood, and the king had decided that they should have a chance of winning their spurs in this African Crusade. They were due to sail from Lisbon on July 25th, 1415. On the 13th Queen Philippa died. Her last thought was for the success of her husband and sons.

"What wind blows so strongly against this side of the house?" she asked.

"It is blowing from the north," answered her sons.

"It is the right wind for your voyage," she murmured, with her last breath. A few days later the motherless princes left Lisbon with their father to win their knighthood.

Prince Henry, though the youngest of the three brothers, was the first to win knighthood. The king's face was bright with joy as Prince Henry approached him, and he welcomed him with the proposal that, as he had borne himself so gloriously, he should receive the honour of knighthood before his brothers. But the prince besought the king that as his brothers Edward and Pedro were older than he was, they might first receive the honour due to them too. The king was pleased with the young man's modesty, and next day the three princes, in full armour, each bearing unsheathed the sword the Queen had given him, were invested with knighthood.

It was three years before Prince Henry returned to live in Portugal. He had shown himself a worthy soldier, and his renown stood high in Europe. He received invitations from the Pope, the Emperor of Germany, and the King of England, to take command of their armies, but Prince Henry had other ideas for his life. He wanted to learn more of the Sea of Darkness over which he had tossed from Lisbon to the coast of Africa. He wanted to know how far that coast on the west extended, what was beyond that great sea across which man had never yet sailed. These things he yearned to know, and these things he now set himself to learn.

CHAPTER 27

PRINCE HENRY, THE SAILOR

"There lies the port—the vessel puffs her sails;
There gloom the dark broad seas."
— TENNYSON.

ONCE back from the wars, the purpose of his life now began to take definite shape. Forsaking the gaiety of court life, he took up his abode on the inhospitable shores of southern Portugal. Amid the sadness of a waste of shifting sand, in a neighbourhood so barren that only a few stunted trees struggled for existence, on one of the coldest, dreariest spots of sunny Portugal, Prince Henry built himself a palace, a chapel, and an observatory.

And here, with the vast Atlantic stretching before him, he devoted himself to the study of the stars, of seamanship, of mathematics. He gathered round him men skilled in the art of drawing maps and men of science. In the neighbouring port of Lagos he built new ships, and trained the Portuguese sailors in the art of seamanship.

"Desire to do well." This was the Prince's motto, and never did man follow any nobler watchword than this.

It was not long before his ships sailed forth in quest of the unknown. Two squires of Prince Henry's household, anxious for fame and wishing to serve their master, set out on an exploring expedition to the coast of West Africa; but being overtaken by a storm they were driven on an island, which they called Porto Santo, as it had saved them from the dangers of the storm. They returned in triumph to Prince Henry, suggesting that a little colony would thrive on their newly found island. The prince took up the idea, and sent out a little settlement of people, to start life on the new island. He also sent with his captain a Spanish pilot who came into his service relating this story:—

Fifty years before an Englishman had run away from Bristol with a very beautiful lady. The boat in which they were flying to France was driven by storms out of its course, finally reaching an island, where the lady died of fright and exposure and her lover a few days later of grief. The sailors who were with them sailed away from the island, only to be wrecked on the coast of Africa and to be thrown into a Moorish prison; but they had told their story to this man, and he was now on his way to act as guide to the island of Madeira. Rediscovered then by the Portuguese, they took it in the name of Prince Henry, and to the Portuguese the islands of Madeira and Porto Santo belong to-day.

Year after year the energetic prince despatched his little ships on the voyages into the unknown sea, ever urging his captains and sailors to venture farther and farther. He gave them new maps and better compasses, and he imparted his enthusiasm to all. To the faint-hearted he gave new courage; those who listened to fables of the sea he rebuked, until one and all determined not to return till they could report some success to their enthusiastic master.

Farther and still farther the ships sailed southward, till at last they reached Cape Bojador, on the west coast of Africa. Here a dangerous surf broke upon the shore, and even the prince's mariners dared not venture farther. There was a popular fable that any man who passed Cape Bojador would be changed from white to black. Men whispered of serpent rocks, sea-monsters, water-unicorns, of sheets of liquid flame and boiling waters!

It was seven years later that the prince's ships reached Cape Blanco, the white headland beyond. Slowly but surely the fables about the great heat were melting away, and men were venturing farther and farther south, but never far from the coast of Africa, never out into the Sea of Darkness. But they brought back gold dust from the coast of Guinea, and they brought back some of the black men as captives to Prince Henry, whose wish was that they should become Christians.

As ship after ship now returned with gold and captives or slaves, Prince Henry's service became more and more popular. No longer had the sailor prince to beg his men to sail forth; all were eager to go and enrich themselves from this newly discovered land. Love of gain was the magic wand that now drew on the Portuguese sailors into the unknown waters, and made them ready for adventure and dangers.

This love of gold and slaves did not appeal to the prince. He still sent out his ships to the west coast, ever hoping for some new light to be shed over the Sea of Darkness, ever longing for some one to discover a pathway through the great waters to distant India.

CHAPTER 28

A FAMOUS VOYAGE

"The Prince, who, Heaven inspired,
To love of useful glory roused mankind,
And in unbounded commerce mixed the world."
—THOMSON.

PERHAPS of all the voyages made in the time of Prince Henry of Portugal, that of the Venetian voyager, Cadamosto, is the most famous; and we have an account of it in his own words. Sailing from Venice to France, Cadamosto was driven by a storm to shelter in the Prince's town near Cape St Vincent. Here he heard of the glorious and boundless discoveries of the Prince's ships, and a passionate desire to see the world and explore the unknown fired him with eagerness to enter the Prince's service.

"No countryman of mine had ever tried the like, and my certainty of winning the highest honour and gain from such a venture made me offer myself," he tells us in his story.

On March 21, 1455, Cadamosto sailed for Madeira, then on to the newly found Canary

Islands—which had been called by Hanno of old, the Islands of the Blessed—and so to the coast of Africa, landing at the white cape, Cape Blanco.

"The natives of Cape Blanco are black as moles, but dress in white flowing robes," says the old traveller and chronicler, "with a turban wound round the head. Indeed, plenty of Arabs are always hovering off the Cape for the sake of trade with Prince Henry's ships, especially in silver, grain, and woven stuffs, slaves and gold."

Coasting on to the southward, he came to the great river Senegal, where the natives were of a colour "something between black and ashes in hue." When first they had seen the ships from Portugal sailing along their coast, they had thought them to be birds coming from afar and cleaving the air with white wings. When the sailors let down the sails and drew the ships to shore, the natives thought they must be fishes, and they stood stupidly on the shore gazing at the new wonder.

On sailed the explorers, south and ever south, till they reached Cape Verde, the most western point of West Africa. The long spell of white sand had now given way to green grass and trees, while native villages were dotted about on the sea-shore. But the Portuguese knew Cape Verde already. Farther south they did not know. So Cadamosto sailed on. They reached the mouth of the river Gambia, and started up the stream to explore farther. But the negroes, "sooty black in colour, dressed in white cotton with helmets on their heads, two white wings on either side and a feather in the middle," came against them. The natives were hostile and unfriendly, so Cadamosto sailed away.

He had already sailed farther south than any of the other Portuguese ships, to within measurable distance of the equator, that imaginary line that divides the world in two parts. Cadamosto did not know that the world was round. He therefore tells Prince Henry on his return, as a curious piece of information, that the Pole Star had sunk so low that it almost touched the sea. Also that they had seen, in their cruise down the African coast, the brilliant group of stars, the Southern Cross, shining through the wonderful June nights.

Cadamosto had done much, but the Prince was not yet satisfied. In 1458 he planned a yet longer voyage, giving the command to his most faithful servant, Diego Gomez. His orders had been simple enough. He was just to sail as far as he could, farther and farther south. Would these explorers never find out what lay beyond this Sea of Darkness? Much had been learnt, but how much more remained to be learnt.

Gomez started forth and sailed beyond Cape Verde, turning due west and coming on the Cape Verde Islands, important to-day as coaling-stations for the large steamers plying between England and Africa and America. He had stories to tell of golden rivers, of gold mines, of ivory tusks and elephant teeth, of houses made of sea-weed covered with straw. He returned to Portugal only in time to be present at the death of his beloved master, Prince Henry.

Still working for the cause he had at heart, his motto, "Desire to do well," ever before him, Prince Henry fell ill. In his own town, near Cape St Vincent, he lay dying, within sound of the great Atlantic rollers, within sight of that vast Sea of Darkness he had failed to fathom.

Perhaps he had done more than ever he dreamt. His energy, his untiring hope, his unwavering purpose and steady determination, had awakened in his countrymen a spirit of enterprise and adventure. He had indeed roused mankind to the love of useful glory, "and in unbounded commerce mixed the world."

CHAPTER 29

THE INVENTION OF PRINTING

"In times ere yet the Press had blest mankind
Perish'd unknown the noblest works of mind."
—M'CREERY.

IT seems strange at first sight to connect the discovery of printing with the discovery of new worlds and the navigation of new seas. But it was just at this time that the invention of printing began to play its large part in the world's history. You can imagine how eagerly men would print in books the accounts of the new lands, and how their hearts would glow as they read of the adventures of the stout-hearted sailors who went on voyages of discovery.

The first book was printed in Europe just ten years before the death of Prince Henry the sailor.

But how did men read books before this? Everything was copied by hand. The old Egyptians, Greeks, and Romans wrote with sharply pointed instruments on sheets of dried skins, or papyrus made from reeds. They wrote on one side only and rolled it up. A long book would be perhaps thirty yards in length. These rolls or books were kept in jars or wooden boxes, a number of which formed a library. They could only be read by the learned: among the people there were no books at all.

Now two countries—Holland and Germany—claim the honour of having invented printing. Nobody quite knows which is right, so here are the two stories.

The men of Holland say that at Haarlem lived a man called Coster. One day he took a walk and cut letters on the bark of a beech-tree. He took them home and printed them on paper to amuse his children. Then he invented a kind of printing ink to put on the blocks of wood, so that they left a mark on the paper. Soon after this he made letters of tin and lead, getting some workmen to come and help him. One night, when Coster was out, one of his workers called John stole all the metal letters, and taking them to Germany, set up a press for himself.

But the Germans say that a man called Gutenberg invented printing at a city on the Rhine,—that he first thought of making pictures in wood and impressing them on paper by means of ink. Then he made letters or type of metal, and after seven years of hard work he printed a copy of the Bible. The secret of the printing-press soon escaped to other parts of Europe, and presses were set up everywhere. Venice, Spain, and France caught the printing fever, while England was not far behind them.

Caxton

The story of how Caxton introduced printing into England is always interesting. News of Gutenberg's discovery reached him, and he went off to Germany to learn the art, knowing what a gain it would be to his country. For thirty-five years he laboured abroad, after which he returned in triumph to England, bringing with him his treasure—a printing-press and a book containing a history of Troy, which he had translated and printed with great labour.

"For my pen is worn, my hand weary, mine eyes dimmed with overmuch looking on the white paper, and my courage not so ready to labour as it hath been," he says pitifully in his preface.

There were no bookbinders in those days; so he bound the book himself, and very clumsy it must have looked. The wooden boards between which the leaves were fastened were as thick as the panel of a door. They were covered with leather. Outside on the cover were large brass nails with big heads, the back was stuck with glue laid on thickly, while the book was fastened with a thick clasp.

"No one can carry it about, much less read it," says one, speaking of the very early books printed by Caxton.

When other men would have ceased work, this man worked on. He printed book after book of English poetry for the people to read and know. He worked on till the day of his death.

"He was not slumbering when his call came, he was still labouring at the work for which he was born."

It was eventide, and the sun was sending its last red streaks of light into Caxton's little workshop, when four men entered, clothed in black, grave, sad, and downcast. The room looked deserted, papers lay about, the ink-blocks were dusty, a thin film had formed over the ink, the machinery looked oily and unused.

The four men drew in their stools, those stools on which they had sat through many a long day working to the end of some manuscript, encouraged by the master who would now direct them no more.

"Companions," said one, "this good work must not stop."

"Who is to carry it on?" asked one sadly.

"I am ready," cried the first speaker.

A cry of joy rose to the lips of the honest workmen.

"Yes," they said, "we will carry on the work briskly in our good master's house. Printing must go forward."

So the faithful workmen carried on the work of their master Caxton, and in the course of the next forty years they had printed four hundred volumes.

So after a time men could read the travels of Marco Polo, the records of the Portuguese explorers, the adventures of Columbus. Maps of the newly discovered regions could be printed, and men's minds opened to the wonders of the world around them.

CHAPTER 30

THE STORMY CAPE

"Over the great windy waters, and over the clear
crested summits,
Unto the sun and the sky. . . come let us go."
—Clough.

Prince Henry was dead; but his work did not die
with him. At the time of his death, in 1460, his ships
had not gone farther than the spot where Hanno had
found his gorillas two thousand years before, but he
had roused in his countrymen the spirit of
adventure, of curiosity in regard to the unknown
seas, which should never die.

Some years after his death the equator was at
last crossed. Wherever they landed it was the custom
of the Portuguese to set up crosses to show that they
had taken possession of the country. Sometimes they
would also carve Prince Henry's motto on the trees,
together with the name they gave to the new land.
Later they took out stone pillars, with the royal arms
sculptured in front surmounted by a cross.

In 1484 one of these stone pillars was set up
by a knight of the king's household at the mouth of

a large river known to us now as the Congo. From the river Niger to this river they found the coast very flat, made up of lagoons and swamps, with a bottom of black mud alive with land-crabs,—hot-beds of African fever.

It would take too long to tell how the King of Congo became a Christian, and commanded all the idols throughout his kingdom to be destroyed. How he received the Portuguese, seated on a throne of ivory raised on a lofty platform; his black and shining skin was uncovered, save for bracelets of copper on his arm, a horse's tail hung from his shoulder, and a cap of palm leaves. He was so impressed with the Portuguese that his children and grandchildren were sent to Lisbon to be educated.

We must now pass on to a great expedition which was fitted out by the King of Portugal for further exploration. Two small ships were made ready, and one Bartholomew Diaz, well known as a daring sailor, was given command. It was fitting that a Diaz should fulfill the ruling desire of the Prince's life. A Diaz had been the first to double Cape Bojador, a Diaz had been the first to reach Cape Verde. A member of the same sea-loving race was to sail first round the extremity of the unknown land of South Africa.

The little party reached the farthest limit of Portuguese exploration, and passed the farthest pillar on the coast of West Africa. Southward still they sailed, till they reached the mouth of the Orange

River, which flows westwards, dividing the Orange River Colony from Cape Colony.

For the next thirteen days they were driven before the wind, due south, the weather growing colder and colder each day, for they were drifting far to the south of South Africa, though they still imagined the coast line ran north and south, as it had done for some time. When the wind abated a little, Diaz steered in the direction he imagined to find land, and was not a little surprised to find himself on a little island in what we now call Algoa Bay. Here he set up a pillar with its cross and gave it the name of Santa Crux, which name still survives. And this was the first land beyond the Cape which was trodden by European feet.

The crews now began to complain: they were worn out and weary, and they were alarmed at the heavy seas through which they were passing. Diaz, his resolute face set eastward toward the unknown, could not bear the thought of returning without further information to bring home. But with one voice the sailors protested. At last it was agreed that they should sail on for three days in the same direction, and if they found no land at the end of that time they would return.

They soon came to the mouth of a large river, now known as the Great Fish River, and as the eastern boundary of Cape Colony. Notwithstanding the interest of the fresh discovery, the crew began their complaints again. They must turn back: they would go no farther. Sadly Diaz was compelled to turn his back on the unknown. When he reached the little island of Santa Cruz he landed and bade farewell to the cross he had set up there with as much sorrow as if he were leaving his child in that wilderness of waters with no hope of ever seeing it again. It seemed as if they had faced all their dangers, undergone all their hardships in vain; and it was in the deepest grief that he sailed to the west on the way home. But as he sailed onwards to the west he came in sight of the mysterious Cape which had been hidden from the eyes of man all through these long ages.

He had some great news to tell the King of Portugal on his return. He had added to the knowledge of the great world, he had made the name of Diaz famous throughout the ages, though he was yet unconscious how important his discovery really was.

"It shall be called the Cape of Storms," he said, when he reached Portugal and made his report to the king.

But the king foresaw the possibility of this being the longed-for way to the East.

"No," he said, "rather the Cape of Good Hope." And it is the Cape of Good Hope to this day.

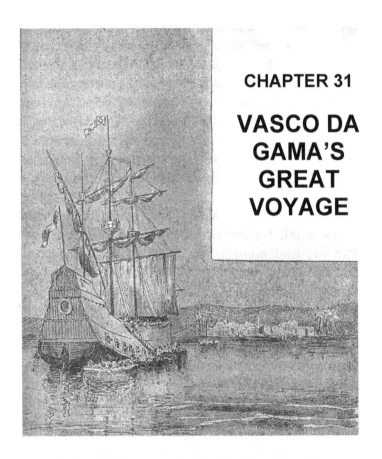

CHAPTER 31

VASCO DA GAMA'S GREAT VOYAGE

"With such mad seas the daring Gama fought
For many a weary day and many a dreadful night;
Incessant labouring round the Stormy Cape,
By bold ambition led."

—THOMSON.

TEN years had passed away since Bartholomew Diaz had made his famous discovery with regard to the south of Africa, and still nothing further had been done. The King of Portugal had prepared three strong ships for an expedition, but he had not found a commander as yet. He was full of care both day and night as to whom he should entrust with so great an enterprise.

One day he was sitting in his hall of business, busy giving orders, when he raised his eyes and saw one of the gentlemen of his household crossing the hall. It was Vasco da Gama, a nobleman of high birth and a well-known sailor. As soon as the king saw him he called him.

"I should rejoice if you would undertake a service which I require of you, in which you must labour much," he said, as his subject knelt before him.

"Sire," answered Vasco da Gama, kissing the king's hand, "I am a servant for any labour that may be, and since my service is required I will perform it so long as my life lasts."

At last, early in the month of July 1497, all was ready. Vasco da Gama on horseback, with all the men of his fleet on foot, richly dressed in liveries and accompanied by all the courtiers, went down to the riverside and embarked in their boats. Reaching their ships, they sailed to the mouth of the Tagus, where they waited for a wind to take them out to sea. Meanwhile an immense crowd gathered on the shore. Men and women were weeping, priests and monks were praying. All were filled with despair for those whom they never expected to see again. Surely they would be buried in the enormous sea-waves that broke around the Stormy Cape whither they were bound. It were better, they cried, to die on shore than so far away from home. The poet

Camoens—called the Virgil of Portugal—tells us that the shining sands were wet with their tears; but the commanders resolutely turned their eyes away to the open sea, and soon, with the royal standard flying from the masthead, the three ships sailed away.

For four long months they sailed to the south, until one November day, at noon, Vasco da Gama sailed before a wind past the formidable Cape, to which the King of Portugal had given the undying name of Good Hope.

It is interesting to note that to-day the voyage from Lisbon to the Cape takes just over a fortnight.

After anchoring for a few days in a little port near the Cape, they again stood out to sea. And now the wind blew with renewed fury, the sea was terrible to behold, and the sailors suffered severely. They besought their commander to turn back.

"Put your trust in the Lord, we shall yet double the Cape," answered Vasco da Gama resolutely. Night and day he worked with the men, enduring all their hardships. As they stood farther out to sea the storms increased, enormous waves dashed over the ships, and every moment they seemed to be going to pieces. Again the sailors and pilots cried to him to have pity on them and to turn the ship back to land.

Then the commander grew angry, and swore that come what might he meant to double the Cape of Good Hope. And the crews worked with fresh vigour when they saw such pluck and perseverance, until after some days they again made land: the seas grew calmer, the winds hushed, and they all knew that the Cape had been doubled at last.

"And great joy fell upon them," says the old Portuguese historian, "and they gave great praise to the Lord on seeing themselves delivered from death."

But their troubles were not over yet. Another storm broke with redoubled fury on them, the seas "rose toward the sky and fell back in heavy showers that flooded the ships."

"Turn back! turn back!" cried the terrified sailors once more, till the commander was forced to answer that he would throw into the sea whosoever spoke of such a thing again. For backwards he would not go, even though he saw a hundred deaths before his eyes. If he did not find that for which he was searching he would not return to Portugal at all.

They now passed Algoa Bay and the little island of Santa Cruz, where Diaz had put up his cross.

As it was Christmas Day, to the coast along which they were sailing they gave the name of Natal. Keeping along the coast, they came presently to the mouth of a large river, up which Vasco da Gama sailed his ships, which were now badly in need of repair. So thankful were the weary mariners for this shelter that they exclaimed, "It is the mercy of the Lord," three times, for which reason they named it the River of Mercy, though to-day it is known as the Zambesi River.

Having repaired the ships and refreshed the men, the commander set up a marble pillar, on which was engraved: "Of the lordship of Portugal, kingdom of Christians."

Then Vasco da Gama called his men together and spoke to them about their want of courage and thoughts of treason, until they wept and promised to serve him to the end. So they weighed anchor and sailed out of the river.

CHAPTER 32

INDIA AT LAST

"O'er Oriental waters now they fly
Upon the Indian seas. . .
And now their chosen task is almost done."
—CAMOENS.

A FEW days' cruising along the eastern coast brought Vasco da Gama to the merchant town of Mozambique, only a few degrees to the south of the equator. Here, however, the chief of the district proved unfriendly, and the Portuguese commander sailed on to Melinda, a trading city on the open coast. It was Easter Day when they anchored in front of the town. News of their coming had spread like wildfire along the coast, and the Indian merchant-ships in port were dressed out with flags in their honour. The king proved a friend in need.

"I will give you pilots," he said, "to take you to the city of Calicut, which is in the country where pepper and ginger grow."

It was August before they were ready to sail. The king was very sad at letting them go, and watched till he could see them no longer.

147

"Lord God have mercy, farewell!" cried the Portuguese sailors as they sailed away into the open sea, leaving the coast of Africa.

For twenty days they sailed to the east, guided by the pilot, and then Vasco da Gama sighted the long faint line of the Indian coast for which he had sailed so far.

"That is India," said the pilot, nodding his head in the direction to which all eyes were strained.

"This is India," echoed the sailors in content, gazing anxiously from the masthead.

It was a tremendous moment for the Portuguese commander when, after three hundred and four days of tossing on the ocean, he arrived at Calicut, on the coast of India. It was more than he could bear, the poet Camoens tells us. Falling down on his knees, he spread his hands abroad to the blue heavens above him, while in the depth of his joy he could find no words. His heroic task was accomplished; he had fulfilled the desire of his king, the dream of Prince Henry of Portugal in days gone by.

People soon flocked, to see the Portuguese ships and sailors, for they soon discovered that Vasco da Gama had gold and silver on board in exchange for the spices of the East. Their king, too, was anxious to hear of the great Christian King of Portugal.

Vasco da Gama, accompanied by twelve of his best-looking sailors, went on shore, taking presents for the Eastern monarch. They took magnificent pieces of scarlet cloth and crimson velvet, a splendid gilt mirror, fifty knives with ivory handles and glittering blades, and other tokens of Portuguese wealth, so that the king swore eternal friendship with his "brother" the King of Portugal, and gave his representatives free leave to buy and sell as they pleased at Calicut. Moreover, he presented da Gama with a beautiful jewelled sword, in a scabbard of velvet and gold, as a solemn pledge of friendship.

Then the Portuguese loaded their ships with the treasures of Calicut, and, enriched with presents from the king, they sailed away for home. With a fair wind and under the guidance of pilots they soon reached Melinda again, sailed past Mozambique, past what we now know as Zanzibar, and rounded the dreaded Cape of Good Hope in fair weather. With shouts of joy they reached Lisbon, exactly two years and eight months after their departure.

The ships had been seen, and the king was waiting to receive Vasco da Gama and eager to hear his news. With his long beard—which had never been cut since he left Lisbon—the successful explorer stepped ashore, and kneeling low before his king he kissed his hand again and again, saying: "Sire, all my hardships have come to an end at this moment."

The news spread far and wide, and great were the rejoicings throughout Portugal, and indeed throughout Europe. "Another road had been discovered to a country which, famed for its riches, had been the envy of Western nations from the earliest times—the dream of every youth of every age from the days of Solomon.

Did we say rejoicings everywhere in Europe? There was one city that did not rejoice at this famous discovery, one city—proud, beautiful, rich—which seemed stunned by the news.

"It is the worst news that ever arrived," they said sadly.

For Venice, amid her waste of waters, was ruined. No longer "did she hold the gorgeous East in fee." Her traffic, her commerce had been taken from her. She had been the first city in Europe

> "till the unwelcome tidings came
> That in the Tagus had arrived a fleet
> From India, from the regions of the sun,
> Fragrant with spices—that a way was found,
> A channel opened, and the golden stream
> Turn'd to enrich another. Then she felt
> Her strength departing, and at last she fell,
> Fell in an instant, blotted out and razed."

CHAPTER 33

THE NEW TRADE-ROUTE

"Then from ancient gloom emerged
The rising world of trade."
—THOMSON.

IT was some time before the rejoicings subsided which had burst over Portugal on the safe return of Vasco da Gama, who had been laden with every possible honour. All eyes now turned to far-off India, even though the way lay through stormy seas, even though it was a well-known fact that Vasco da Gama had lost his brother and more than half his men in the perilous voyage. The pepper, cloves, cinnamon, ginger, and mace brought back from Calicut had yielded immense profits at home, and men were eager to go and get more.

So the king fitted out another expedition, and gave the command of it to Pedro Cabral, with whom Bartholomew Diaz, the original discoverer of the Cape, was to sail. Thirteen ships were well supplied and manned. Monks were to sail with the fleet in order to teach Christianity to the native Indians, while 1200 picked soldiers went in case of trouble.

151

The fleet sailed from Lisbon on March 9, 1500. Cabral guided his ships past the Cape Verde Islands safely, and then for some reason, perhaps driven by stormy weather, he took a westerly course that he knew. On and on he sailed, till a month later he found himself on an unknown coast in an unknown land. It was Brazil, in South America. But he named it Santa Cruz, and took formal possession of it in the name of the King of Portugal. Sending a ship home with the news, and some gorgeous paroquets from the country, he then made his way to India.

Two months after he left Lisbon he reached the Cape. As the ships sailed round the southern point they encountered a terrific storm. The waves rolled mountains high, the wind whistled and shrieked, and four ships foundered. Among them was one commanded by Diaz, the man who had revealed the secret of the Cape kept through so many long ages. For him it was indeed a Cape of Storms. With six ships only, Cabral pushed on to Mozambique, and thence to Calicut. He entered into a commercial treaty with the Indians, but treachery was at work and a number of Portuguese were massacred.

Cabral returned to Lisbon with only three ships out of the thirteen that started, for he lost one on the reefs near Melinda, laden with spices from India.

"Sire, my inclination prompts me to make another voyage," said Vasco da Gama one day after the return of Cabral, whose doubtful fortune had disappointed the king. "Wherefore I entreat your Highness to allow it for your service."

The king was delighted, and Vasco da Gama was soon afloat again with thirteen ships, ten of which were ships of war, for this was to be an expedition of revenge on the King of Calicut for his double dealing with the Portuguese.

"I feel in my heart a great wish to go and make havoc of the King of Calicut, so that I may take vengeance on him, and that your Highness may be much pleased," were among Gama's last words to his Christian sovereign.

It was a sorry way to carry the message of peace to the natives of India.

With banners and standards, and crosses of Christ on every sail, the ships started on March 25, 1502. They had a tremendous storm while rounding the Cape, which separated the fleet, but all save one turned up at Mozambique. It was August before they reached Melinda, where the king received Gama as an old friend, and loaded him with presents. Sailing on to India, the Portuguese commander took a horrible revenge on the Indian traders, whom he wished to impress with the power and the majesty of the great Christian monarch whom he served.

He ordered that some eight hundred merchants, captured in peaceful commerce, should have their hands, ears, and noses cut off, their feet tied together, and be placed in heaps on board ship, covered over with dry mats and leaves. Then the ship was set on fire with her sails set, and so drifted to shore.

No wonder the King of Calicut prepared a fleet to sail against this cruel Portuguese commander. But he was no match for well-equipped ships from the West. More revenge and cruelty followed, until in the end Vasco da Gama terrified the merchants into submission, left a Portuguese colony on the Indian coast, and sailed for home with ten ships laden with wealth from India.

Great were the king's rejoicings when he saw Vasco da Gama again.

"You shall be Admiral of the Indian Seas for ever," he cried.

Some years later Vasco da Gama went out to India again, and there he died, far away in the country he had discovered for Portugal.

He had rendered great services to his king and to the whole world, but the glory of his fame will ever be stained by the remembrance of his cruel oppression of the traders on the western coast.

CHAPTER 34

GOLDEN GOA

"Where the gorgeous East, with richest hand,
Showers on her kings barbaric pearls and gold."
—MILTON.

WHILE Vasco da Gama was on his way back from India to Portugal, another expedition left Lisbon under a man who was destined to be one of the wisest and justest of Portuguese rulers in that far-off country. Affonso d'Albuquerque was brought up at the Court of the King of Portugal, and taught with the king's own sons. He had shown himself fearless in battle, chivalrous in action, and wise in times of peace. It was natural, therefore, that he should be selected to take charge of three ships—bound, as all ships from Portugal were bound at this time, for the coast of India.

He soon returned from a successful voyage to lay before the king his idea of closing other routes to this rich country of India, so that Portugal alone could get its treasure. Up to this time ships manned by the Moors and Arabs had taken the treasure to Ormuz, a rich city on the Persian Gulf, whence it was taken to the mouth of the Euphrates, across Asia Minor on caravans to the coast, and shipped thus to Europe. Or it was taken by ship to Suez, thence by caravan to Cairo, and down the Nile to Alexandria, whence ships from Venice distributed it to Europe.

"This must be stopped," said Albuquerque, jealous for his country's wealth.

And with this object in view he again started for the East. He sailed to Ormuz, "the richest jewel set in the ring of the world," as the old writer called it, and grasped the importance of getting the town to stop the trade between India and Europe that way. Having arranged matters to his satisfaction with the King of Ormuz, and planned a Portuguese fort, he cruised about on the shores of Arabia, establishing the power of Portugal everywhere.

Then he sailed to India, where by royal orders he was made Governor.

One of his first acts was the capture of the town of Goa, to the north of Calicut, for the commercial capital of the Portuguese in India. The island of Goa was formed by the mouths of two rivers, which fitted it easily for defence. There was safe anchorage, and it had long been visited by the merchants of many nations. The capture of Goa was not easy, but Albuquerque was determined to take it, and finally did so. He then forbade the towns of Calicut and others to buy and sell, so that Goa— "Golden Goa" as she was called—became one of the most splendid and wealthy cities on the face of the earth for the next hundred years. Ships laden with the wealth of India sailed from Goa to Lisbon, and no one was allowed to trade with India except by leave of the Portuguese at this time.

On the east coast of Africa to-day we have names surviving from these times. Algoa Bay—to Goa—was a stopping-place for ships journeying to this great Indian island of Goa; while Delagoa Bay, farther north and still belonging to the Portuguese, was the other stopping-place back from Goa, as its name implies.

Early in the year 1513 Albuquerque sailed out of the harbour of Goa, bound for the Red Sea, with a fleet of twenty ships.

Now the Arabs living on the shores of the Red Sea greatly resented the Portuguese taking away their trade with India, and when they heard that the fleet was already sailing for Aden, a town at the narrow straits leading into the Red Sea, they lit fires on the hills beyond, to lure the ships to destruction. But the Portuguese steered safely into harbour, and after an unsuccessful attempt to storm the city, set fire to the ships and sailed on. Albuquerque explored the shores of the Red Sea, but did not reach Suez, the goal he had in view. It is, however, an interesting point to be noted here, that the route from Europe to India that Albuquerque tried to close is to-day the short highway for ships to the far East. For in the year 1869 the Suez canal was opened, 100 miles in length, which joined the Mediterranean Sea with the Red Sea.

Albuquerque now sailed back past Aden to the mouth of the Persian Gulf in order to reduce Ormuz. For the old king was dead, and the Portuguese fortress was not finished. The great governor of India and conqueror of Goa soon made his presence felt. Ormuz was conquered and the fortress completed. The fame of Albuquerque was now at its height, but his health was broken.

Day by day he grew worse. Such was his fame that people from all over the country came to the fortress at Ormuz to try and get a sight of him. If perchance he rode out on horseback, so great was the crowd that he could hardly go forward. At last he felt sure the end was nearing. He wished to reach Goa, the city he had conquered, the city he loved.

So one day, early in November 1515, a ship sailed away from Ormuz bearing the dying man back to India. A deep sorrow awaited him. He lived to learn that the king had appointed another governor to succeed him.

"In bad repute with men because of the king, and in bad repute with the king because of men," cried the dying man, holding up his hands. "It were well that I were gone."

Outside Goa, the great capital of Indian commerce, he died; and so great was the crying and weeping on all sides, that it seemed as if "the very river of God was being poured out," cried the old chronicler.

CHAPTER 35

CHRISTOPHER COLUMBUS

"Eighteen long years of waste,
seven in your Spain Lost. . ."
—TENNYSON (Columbus).

ONE day, in the year 1484, a tall, strongly built man of commanding presence stood before the King of Portugal at the Court of Lisbon. All men of adventurous spirit were drawn to Portugal in these days, for though Prince Henry was long since dead, the enthusiasm he had aroused lived on in his heirs.

Portuguese sailors had already passed the equator,—had even reached the Congo, on the west coast of Africa; but the Cape was yet shrouded in mystery when Christopher Columbus stood before the king. Little did that king realise the strength of the man who now stood before him. He could not read those keen blue-grey eyes, kindling with eager interest, as the Italian unfolded his great, his wonderful plan.

"Sail to the West and the East will be found."

159

Such words seemed at first the words of a madman. Columbus explained his idea to the king. He told him of the long years he had worked at his scheme, how sure he felt that there was a shorter way to the East—to the land of the Great Khan of Marco Polo fame—than by Africa. The world was surely round. If Asia could be reached by sailing east, surely it could be reached by going west. If the king would grant him ships and money, he was ready to go and see.

The king listened with interest, and referred the plan to some of his learned men. They called Columbus a dreamer, and scoffed at his dreams. Finally they persuaded the king to an ungenerous act. They got from Columbus the plans of his proposed voyage, and while they kept him in suspense awaiting the king's decision, they despatched some ships off privately to investigate the matter.

Away sailed the ships to the Cape Verde Islands. But the weather grew stormy, the pilots trembled at the sight of an unlimited waste of wild tumbling waves, and, losing heart, they returned to tell the king of their failure.

When Columbus heard of this injustice he straightway left Portugal. He would have nothing more to do with a country which could serve him thus. He took his little son, Diego, by the hand, and went to Spain.

One day, says an old story, a stranger walked up to the gate of an ancient monastery, which stood on a solitary height overlooking the southern sea-coast of Spain. The stranger, who was leading a small child, stopped to ask for bread and water, for the boy was hungry.

Columbus and Diego.

It was Christopher Columbus and little Diego. They were taken in and fed, and the friar of the monastery was much struck with the grand ideas put forth by this stranger within his gates. He strongly advised him to go to the Spanish Court, where he would find a king and queen—Ferdinand and Isabella—who would certainly listen to his plans. So leaving little Diego behind, he set forth to try and get an audience with the King and Queen of Spain.

Now the Moors, against whom the Cid had fought four centuries before, were still reigning in the southern part of Spain called Granada. All the country was taken up with a great war that was going on between the Christian monarchs, Ferdinand and Isabella, and the Moorish king of Granada, and Columbus could get no one to listen to his great scheme.

Weeks and months, even years, went by, and the Spanish monarchs could spare no time to give audience to the future discoverer of America. It was not till the end of the year 1491 that he was summoned to the king and queen at their camp outside the town of Granada, which they were besieging. So poor was he by this time that the queen sent him money to get clothes suitable to appear at Court.

Here was the great chance for which he had so longed. But though poor, Columbus was proud. He believed in his plan, and he demanded great things. He must be made admiral and viceroy of all the new seas and countries that he should discover, and have one-tenth part of all the gains. His demands were laughed at, and he was dismissed by the Spanish Court.

Mounting his mule, Columbus rode sadly away. Once more he had failed.

But his friends could not bear to see him treated thus. They approached Queen Isabella. In glowing colours they put before her the great possibilities of the scheme, until she exclaimed with fervour: "I will undertake the enterprise for my own crown of Castile, and will pledge my jewels to raise the necessary funds."

A messenger rode hard after Columbus, brought him back to the queen, and all was settled for the great voyage.

Spain, after all, was to have the glory and honour of sending Columbus to discover the New World.

CHAPTER 36

THE LAST OF THE MOORS

"If earth contains a paradise
It is beneath Granada's skies."

WHILE Columbus is preparing for his first voyage to the West, let us take a look at the country he is now serving, and tell again the picturesque story of the fall of Granada.

In the days of the Cid the Moors had occupied a large part of Spain, but since then they had been driven nearer and nearer to the coast, till only the beautiful kingdom of Granada was left to them. It was this stronghold that the King of Spain was besieging when Columbus laid before him his great plan of discovery. And with the fall of Granada the long reign of the Moors in Spain was over.

This beautiful city stood on two lofty hills. One of them was crowned by the famous palace and fortress of the Alhambra, celebrated for its marble colonnades, its domes, and ceilings glowing with colour. While cities in the plains panted with heat, fresh breezes played through the marble halls of the Alhambra. So pure was the air, so beautiful was the

164

earth in this spot, that the Moors used to imagine that their prophet Mohammed dwelt in that part of the heaven that hung over Granada.

Ferdinand and Isabella were Christians, and they could not bear the Moors to hold any part of their Christian country in Spain. One day they sent a Spanish messenger to demand tribute from the King of the Moors.

"Tell your king," cried the fierce Moor bitterly, "that the kings of Granada who used to pay tribute to the King of Spain are dead. Our mint coins nothing now but blades of swords and heads of lances."

The Spanish messenger rode away, noting as he rode the strength of this last stronghold of the Moors.

Ferdinand now sent to demand a complete surrender of the town. He received back a firm answer that the Moors would sooner die than yield up their beautiful city to Christian warriors, and Ferdinand prepared for war.

The din of arms now filled the city. Under Muza, one of the proudest of the Moors, the men of Granada gathered. They would defend their town even with their lives. Ferdinand's plan was to devastate the plains round Granada and so starve the city into surrender. He laid waste the fields of waving corn, he burnt the lovely gardens and orchards which were the pride and joy of the Moors, but still the standard of Mohammed waved defiance to the Christian king from the red towers of the Alhambra.

"How is thy strength departed, O Granada," lamented the Moors; "how is thy beauty withered, O city of groves and fountains. The commerce that once thronged thy streets is at an end; the merchant no longer hastens to thy gates with luxuries of foreign lands."

They prepared for attack from the Spaniards; but in the hour of her despair Granada was no easy city to take, and Ferdinand knew his only hope of success lay in starving out the people.

At last famine began to make itself felt among the Moors. There was no harvest to look to, the orchards and gardens were burnt. Gloomy indeed was their outlook.

"What shall we do?" asked the king hopelessly.

"Surrender," answered the Moors.

"Do not talk of surrender," cried the brave Muza. "Our means are not yet exhausted. We have one source of strength remaining—it is our despair. Let us rouse the mass of the people and arm them. Rather let us fall in the defence of our city than survive to surrender."

But his fiery words fell on the ears of broken-hearted men. Heroic as they were, the despairing Moors turned a deaf ear to them.

"Surrender, surrender," they moaned.

And the king listened to them, and yielded. He sent to Ferdinand to treat for terms. At the end of seventy days the city was to surrender. When the Moors found that the moment had come when they—the conquerors of Spain—must be blotted out for ever as a nation, they gave way to piteous tears.

"Leave this weeping to the women and children," cried Muza. "We are men, we have hearts—not to shed tender tears, but drops of blood. Let us die defending our liberty; let it not be said the nobles of Granada feared to die."

But the careworn Moors were beyond Muza's appeal. It was hopeless to contend longer. He rose angrily as the king signed the agreement, strode gloomily through the marble courts, armed himself, and, mounting his favourite war-horse, rode forth from the gates of Granada. He was never heard of more.

The weary days passed by, until the last day came. The royal treasures were packed on mules, and before dawn a weeping procession of downcast Moors, with their king, passed from the beautiful city they would never see again. The sun was shining above the snowy peaks behind the city, when the King and Queen of Spain rode across the plain to take possession of Granada. The joyful procession met the unhappy Moorish king, who yielded up the keys.

"These keys are the last relics of the Moorish Empire in Spain," he said miserably; and as he

THE DISCOVERY OF NEW WORLDS

journeyed on in gloomy silence, the shouts of the victorious Spaniards fell on his ears. As he reached the hill which commanded the last view of Granada, he stopped. The sun caught the silver cross of the Christians as it sparkled on the watch-tower of the Alhambra.

"God is great," he groaned, bursting into tears, "God is great. When did such misfortunes equal mine?"

So did the Moors leave Spain for ever.

CHAPTER 37

DISCOVERY OF THE NEW WORLD

"Lord of the lordly sea,
Earth's mightiest captain he."
—WATSON.

THE year 1492 was a proud year for Spain, when the last Moorish stronghold had fallen and Christopher Columbus had started on his great voyage of discovery.

He had had difficulties in making the preparations for his start. The Spanish sailors looked on the expedition with horror, and the commander as a madman. It was early on the morning of August 3 that the little fleet of three ships sailed forth from a southern Spanish port. A more unwilling crew never left land. As the last speck of Spain vanished from their backward gaze, and only the wide waters of the Atlantic stretched before them, the men burst into tears as they thought of the home and friends they never expected to see again.

Ten days' sail brought them to the Canary Islands. And now, instead of turning south, as the Portuguese sailors were doing, Columbus steered to the west, a direction in which no man had steered before.

As day after day, week after week, passed by, bringing no sight of land, but only a wide expanse of waters, the crew grew more and more discontented. They complained and murmured against their admiral, until they nearly broke into open mutiny.

"We are in seas where never yet man ventured before," they said among themselves; "are we to sail till we perish?"

Surely it would be wiser to throw the admiral into his unknown sea and turn the ships for home. And Columbus? He knew all this: but he set his face resolutely forward, he never wavered from his course, his faith in his great plan never left him. He tried to stir his men to interest themselves in the strange land to which he was guiding them, and offered a large reward to the man who should first see land.

So they sailed on, till at last it became evident that land was not very far off. Birds came singing about the ships, weeds were seen floating in the water, and a branch of thorn with red berries was borne past them. All became eager enough now.

It was the evening of October 7—two months since they had left home. When the crews collected as usual to sing their evening hymn,

Columbus spoke to them. Land was very near now, he said; God had been good to bring them in safety thus far; let every man watch, for their reward was at hand.

Not an eye closed that night. As darkness came on Columbus took his watch on the highest place in the ship, while his eye searched again and again the dusky horizon. About ten o'clock he saw a glimmering light far away. Every eye was fixed on it, till at two o'clock in the early morning a gun, fired from one of the other ships, proved him right. Land had been seen. Eagerly, impatiently, they awaited daylight.

When the sun rose on the morning of the 8th there stretched before the earnest eyes of the resolute commander a beautiful island, green, cool, and well wooded.

They had reached the Bahama Islands, off the coast of America; but Columbus thought they were off the coast of Asia, never realising that a whole country stretched between him and Asia.

Taking the royal standard of Spain, and throwing a crimson cloak over his coat of mail, he rowed to shore. As he stepped on to the newly found land, he threw himself on to his knees, kissed the strange new earth, and praised God with tears of joy. Then rising, he drew his sword, and took possession of the island in the name of Ferdinand and Isabella of Spain.

The men now thronged round him, kissing his hands, begging forgiveness, assuring him of their unbounded trust in him.

And Columbus? He had accomplished the work of his life. The thoughts and plans and dreams of a lifetime had been crowned with success. He had discovered a new world of vast importance. This much he knew and no more.

Natives now came up to the Spaniards. They had gazed for some time at the shining armour, the swarthy skins, long beards, and splendid dress of these strangers to their shores. Now, by signs, they told the Spaniards of more land to the south and west. So away sailed Columbus, finding another island, now called Cuba, just off the coast of Florida, in North America.

It was all so beautiful here. Birds of brilliant colours never ceased to sing, clear streams and rivers flowed to the sea. There were stately forests, sweet-smelling flowers, all under a deep blue sky.

From island to island they cruised, discovering many things of which no man had dreamt before. In Cuba they discovered tobacco and potatoes, two products hitherto unknown in Europe.

But now Columbus wanted to get back to Spain to tell his wondrous news. On the way home a terrible storm burst over the Atlantic, and it seemed for a time as if the little Spanish ships must perish with all on board. But they triumphantly weathered the gales, and sailed into the Spanish harbour of Palos just seven months after their departure.

Columbus's Ship.

CHAPTER 38

THE WEST INDIES

"The city deck'd herself
To meet me, roar'd my name: the king, the queen
Bade me be seated, speak and tell them all
The story of my voyage, . . .
And when I ceas'd to speak, the king, the queen
Sank from their thrones and melted into tears,
And knelt and lifted hand and heart and voice
In praise to God, who led me thro' the waste."
—TENNYSON.

SEVEN months had passed since Columbus had sailed from Spain in the dim light of that summer morning. Now he was back. Through tempestuous seas and raging winter gales he had guided his ship well, and Spain knew how to do him honour. His journey from the coast to the Court was like a royal progress. The wonderful news of his return had spread far and wide. The roads were lined with excited villagers, the air was rent with shouts of joy. His entrance into the city was not unlike the triumph decreed by the old Romans to their heroes.

First came six natives, brought back from the islands by Columbus, painted in their savage fashion and decorated with ornaments of gold. Bearers followed, with forty parrots and other birds of strange and brilliant colouring, skins of unknown animals, and priceless curious plants.

On horseback rode Christopher Columbus, his stately figure and grey hair marking him out among the mounted chivalry of Spain. The king and queen rose to receive him, and as he stooped to kiss their hands they bade him be seated—a rare honour in that proud Spanish Court.

Not Spain only, but the whole civilised world, was filled with wonder and delight. The opinion of Columbus was adopted: Cuba lay off the coast of Asia; the island was not far from the land of the Great Khan, Marco Polo's country. It lay in the Indian Seas, together with the other newly discovered island. So they were called the West Indies, which name they have borne ever since, though we know now they are not near Asia at all, but close to the coast of South America.

The departure of Columbus on his second voyage was a brilliant contrast to the gloomy start of a year ago. The bay of Cadiz—the Gades of the old Phœnicians—was full of his ships. The 1500 men who were to sail with him were in highest spirits, for were they not bound for the golden realms of the New World, where wealth, wonder, and enjoyment awaited them?

The start was made on September 25, 1493. Two months later Columbus sailed into the beautiful bay of Hayti, an island he had discovered on his first voyage, lying to the south of Cuba. Here he built a town, and called it Isabella, after the Queen of Spain. Sailing on, he found a new island, which the natives called Jamaica. Still he had dreams of finding India, perhaps sailing home by the Cape of Good Hope, as yet only dimly shadowed by Bartholomew Diaz. But his ships were leaky, his men proved troublesome, he himself grew ill, and they were obliged to put back to the new colony of Isabella to recruit. More troubles here. Complaints broke from the new settlers. They had thought they would become rich men at once, and this was impossible. Columbus was not a Spaniard like themselves, but an Italian. Reports reached the ears of the king and queen in Spain. Discontented colonists returned, spreading false stories of the cruelty of the new Viceroy and the condition of the newly found country.

A Spaniard was sent out to the new colony to inquire if this was all true or not, and to take charge of Isabella. Columbus was away when he arrived, on an exploring expedition. He returned to find himself accused of tyranny, cruelty, deceit, and failure. Columbus made up his mind to return at once to Spain and see the king and queen.

The ships were ready to depart when a terrific storm swept the island of Hayti, sinking ships in the harbour. The natives were overwhelmed, for never had they known such a tremendous storm. Out of the wrecks a new ship had to be made, and another repaired, to carry Columbus home. Meanwhile a rich gold mine was discovered inland. This would be good news for Columbus to carry to Spain. For himself, he made sure he had found the Ophir of the ancients—possibly the very mines from which King Solomon procured the gold for the building of the temple of Jerusalem.

It was June 11, 1496, before he found himself again in the harbour of Cadiz. People had crowded down to greet the great discoverer, but instead of a joyous crew, flushed with new success and rich with the spoils of the golden Indies, a feeble train of wretched men crawled on shore—thin, miserable, and ill. Columbus himself was dressed as a monk, in a long gown girded with a cord. His beard was long and unshaven. The whole man was utterly broken down with all he had been through.

The king and queen listened to his explanation, and soon preparations were set on foot to send him out again to the new country.

CHAPTER 39

COLUMBUS IN CHAINS

"When shall the world forget
Thy glory and our debt,
Indomitable soul."
—WATSON (Columbus).

WHILE Columbus was pleading his cause in Spain and preparing for another expedition, Vasco da Gama was sailing for the first time round the dreaded Cape. And it is curious to think that he made the coast of India just ten days before Columbus sailed for the third time for the New World he had discovered. Thus India and the East were to Portugal, at this time, what America and the West were to Spain.

It was in the month of May 1498 when Columbus started off again. After passing the Cape Verde Islands he steered to the south-west, hoping to make for new islands to the south of Cuba and Hayti. He soon found himself in a dead-calm sea. The air was like a furnace, the tar melted from off the ships, the seams yawned, the salt meat went bad, the sailors lost strength and spirits, and Columbus himself lay in raging fever. He had reluctantly to alter his course and steer to the north again.

It was three months since they left Spain, when a sailor from the mast-head saw land. Three mountains seemed to rise up out of the sea; and when Columbus reached the island—for island it was—he called it the Trinity, or Trinidad, which name it bears to-day. Then he sailed between this island and the mainland, little knowing that the land was South America, the great continent for which he had been searching all these long years.

Here he obtained a large quantity of pearls from the natives, and he would gladly have spent longer in the neighbourhood, but his stores were at an end, and he himself was nearly blind with eyes worn out with over-watching and anxiety. Passing through the narrow straits between Trinidad and the mainland, he was nearly wrecked. A foaming roaring current rushed through the narrow passage, which Columbus called the Dragon's Mouth.

But he reached Hayti in safety, to be received with open arms by his brother, who had been ruling over the little Spanish colony in his absence. Things had gone ill with the colony, and Columbus did not improve matters by his presence. He was no statesman, no leader of men. He punished the leading colonists, he made slaves of the natives, and took other measures for reducing the colony to order. Complaints again reached the king and queen, who at once sent out a Spaniard to replace Columbus in his command. This high-handed knight at once put Columbus in chains and shut him up in a fortress. One day an officer entered, and Columbus thought they were going to hang him.

"Whither are you taking me?" he asked hopelessly.

"To the ship, your excellency, to embark," was the answer.

"To embark? Do you speak the truth?" asked the admiral of the ocean sea.

"Indeed it is true," answered the officer.

He was taken on board a ship, and in October 1500 sailed once more for home. The captain would have taken off his chains, but Columbus refused.

"No," he said proudly; "by royal order I am in chains. I will wear them till my king and queen order them to be taken off, when I will keep them as relics of the reward of my service."

It is said that the eyes of Queen Isabella filled with tears as the white-haired discoverer stood before her, his face lined with suffering. As for Columbus himself, his long pent-up feelings overcame him, and in an agony of weeping he threw himself at her feet.

Once more he was restored to favour; once more he was given ships to sail again for the new country: but there was no more success in store for Christopher Columbus.

His fourth voyage revealed little new. Driven to seek shelter in the harbour of Hayti, he was refused an entrance by the new governor of the island which he—Columbus—had given to the world. Still his dream never left him. He must reach India, he must find the home of Marco Polo's Great Khan, before he died. He still believed that Cuba was the coast of Asia. And he was to die in this belief.

He had shown the way to the West: it was for others to follow. Hardships, disaster, failure—these were now to be his lot. He returned to Spain a broken man, only to hear the news that the Queen of Spain was dead. She had befriended him when no one else was ready to believe in him, she had understood his sufferings and mingled her tears with his. Now he was friendless. Not only this—he was penniless.

"I receive nothing of the money that was due to me," he says pitifully, as he nears the end; "I live by borrowing. After twenty years of toil and peril, I do not own a roof in Spain."

> "I, lying here, bedridden and alone,
>   Cast off, put by, scouted by court and king,
>   The first discoverer starves."

And so Christopher Columbus sailed forth on his "one last voyage."

He died in May 1506, still dreaming of some vaster Spain he yet might give his adopted country,—"the mightiest, wealthiest realm on earth,"—but all unconscious of the great continent of America, which he had made known to the wondering world.

CHAPTER 40

A GREAT MISTAKE

"The lamp burns low, and through the casement bars
  Grey morning glimmers feebly."

—BROWNING.

"THE great Columbus of the heavens,"—so they called Copernicus, the man who about this time discovered as much about the heavens as Columbus had discovered about the earth. For he found that for all these hundreds of years the whole world had been labouring under a wrong idea about the relation of the earth to the sun,—that the wise and clever men of the past had made a great mistake.

Let us see how this man, Copernicus, discovered the truth.

He was born in distant Poland in the year 1473, just about the time when Prince Henry was busy sending out his Portuguese ships into the Sea of Darkness to find the Cape of Good Hope. When he died—an old man of seventy—Vasco da Gama had found the route to India by the Cape, Columbus had discovered America, Balboa had seen the Pacific Ocean, Magellan had sailed round the world, Cortes had conquered Mexico, and Pizarro had conquered Peru. Men were stretching out their hands for a new earth. This man was to show them a new heaven.

As a boy, Copernicus showed great taste for mathematics and astronomy; and such was his ability that he was sent to Rome to lecture on the stars to the students there. But he soon returned to his home in Poland, for he wished to learn more of the sun, moon, and stars, and to have plenty of time for quiet study. The old astronomers told him that the earth was fixed and motionless, while the sun, moon, and stars moved right round her once every twenty-four hours. In this way they accounted for the changes of night and day, darkness and light.

But this theory did not satisfy Copernicus at all. He was convinced that the old astronomers were wrong. And yet it seemed almost easier to believe that he himself was wrong than that all the clever men who had lived before him had made such a mistake. He worked on and on, pondering, observing, making instruments to try and learn more about the heavenly bodies. At last one day there flashed into his mind this idea. Was it possible that the earth was not fixed and motionless after all? Could it be that the earth moved round the sun, and the sun did not move round the earth?

There was an old Greek philosopher who had lived twenty centuries before, and he had hinted that this was the case. Eagerly Copernicus turned to the old Greek writings. With breathless interest he read again of this suggestion that the earth was not fixed, but moving. Feverishly he worked out his observations on this new theory. It is impossible to imagine the amazement and wonder that filled his mind at the discovery of what is to us to-day a well-known fact. We know now that day and night are caused by the earth revolving on its own axis, turning first one side to the sun and then the other; that the earth, apparently so still and motionless beneath our feet, is really moving round and round at a pace that no train can touch for speed.

As this fact burst on the mind of Copernicus, he was awestruck.

He did not make known his discovery at once: he went on working as before, until he became more and more certain that he was right.

When at last he proclaimed his discovery, he was simply laughed at.

As Columbus had been ridiculed for suggesting that the world was round as he stood before the King and Queen of Spain, so Copernicus was scoffed at for his suggestion that the earth moved round the sun.

"He is suffering from delusions of too childish a character," cried his friends.

> "Think how absurd a jest,—
> That neither heavens nor stars do turn at all,
> Nor dance about this great round Earthy Ball,
> But the Earth itself, this massy globe of ours,
> Turns round but once every twice twelve hours."

So scoffed the poets at the man who had toiled for thirty-six long years at his theory before he gave it to the world.

Fortunately some believed in him, and persuaded him to write a book about it. While he sat day after day writing his book, he suffered many things from ignorant folk, who looked with horror on this man who affirmed that the earth was moving. When at last it was finished Copernicus was an old man, worn out with work, anxiety, and pain. One of his faithful disciples took the precious manuscript to a printing-press at Nuremberg.

But when it became known that the book was actually being printed, all the ignorance and jealousy of his countrymen burst forth. Men tried to get at the press to destroy the book. The printers worked with a loaded pistol ready at their side, while two faithful friends guarded the manuscript day and night.

The excitement of the author was intense: it utterly broke him down. He became very ill, and it was feared that he would never see his book in print. It was the 23rd of May 1543. Copernicus was sinking rapidly. Silence reigned in the sick-room, where he lay dying. His book had not come.

Suddenly the flicker of a smile lit up the old man's face. The sound of a horse's hoofs was coming nearer and ever nearer. Another minute and the printed book containing his life's work was gently laid in his almost nerveless hands. His wasted fingers grasped the volume for which he had longed

Copernicus.

and waited. He had not lived his life in vain. Sinking back with a deep sigh of satisfaction, he murmured faintly the pathetic words, only caught by those near him: "Lord, now lettest thou thy servant depart in peace."

CHAPTER 41

FOLLOW THE LEADER

"Go from the east to the west,
    as the sun and the stars direct thee;
Go with the girdle of man,
    go and encompass the earth,
Not for the gain of the gold—for the getting,
    the hoarding, the having—
But for the joy of the deed,
    but for the Duty to do."
                                    —CLOUGH.

ONCE Columbus had led the way to the New World, it was easy enough for others to follow. He had resolutely plunged across the unknown Sea of Darkness and found land beyond. There is a story told of him that shows that he, too, knew how great had been the plunge.

He was sitting at dinner when a Spaniard, somewhat jealous of his fortune, suggested that if he—Columbus—had not found the new country, some other Spaniard might easily have done so. Columbus said nothing, but taking an egg, he asked if any one present could make it stand. All tried, but in vain. Then Columbus took the egg, and having

188

cracked one end on the table, he stood it up. All saw his meaning. Once the thing was done, it was no hard matter to do it again.

Columbus had just returned from his discovery of land across the Atlantic—though he had not found the mainland of the new world—when John Cabot started off, full of enthusiasm, for a voyage across the ocean.

Like Columbus, he was an Italian by birth, and, like him, Cabot had applied to the two Courts of Portugal and Spain for ships and money. But finally he was sailing from England. Bristol, the chief seaport of England at this time, traded with Venice and Lisbon, and her merchants had already ventured some distance out into the broad Atlantic. It was from Bristol that John Cabot and his son Sebastian sailed one bright May morning in the famous year 1497, a year which they were to make yet more famous by their further discoveries. They sailed with one small ship and only eighteen sailors, and soon found themselves tossing on the yet dimly known ocean. By the end of June they had fallen in with land. It was really New-foundland, off the coast of North America, but they thought it was China—the land of the Great Khan.

Never since the old Viking days had white men been seen on these shores, and they had left no trace. By July the Cabots were home again, telling the King of England, Henry VII., of their good fortune. It is amusing to find the thrifty king bestowing on "him that found the new isle" the famous grant of £10! But other honours were heaped upon him. He was called the Grand Admiral, and dressed in silk; and we hear further that "the English ran after him like madmen." Again and again after this Sebastian Cabot sailed to North America, ever bringing back news of fresh lands discovered and fresh wonders seen; but as yet no colonists felt tempted to settle in the bleak north. The inhospitable shores of Labrador offered no attraction, and it was a long time before any use was made of these discoveries.

Neither did Cabot himself ever know the value of them, but he died, as his great leader had died, still thinking that he had found the coast of China, the golden Cathay of Marco Polo.

The story of Amerigo Vespucci, who also followed his leader to the new country, is curious, for it was named after him America. He had made several voyages to the West, while Columbus was yet going backwards and forwards to his newly discovered lands. He had sailed under a Spaniard through the Dragon's Mouth between Trinidad and the mainland of South America, had found a village—forty-four large houses built on huge tree-trunks and connected by bridges: it was like the Italian Venice rising out of her lagoons, and is known to-day as Venezuela or little Venice.

But it was not till after the death of Columbus, after Amerigo Vespucci had been many times to the West and coasted down the east coast of South America, much farther than Columbus had ever done, that the idea began to dawn on men that this land was neither Asia nor Africa, that it was not the land of the Great Khan nor the India of Vasco da Gama, but a new continent altogether.

"It is proper to call it a new world," says Amerigo Vespucci. "And why? Because these lands were unknown to the men of old. They said over and over again that there was no land south of the equator. But this last voyage of mine has proved them wrong, since in southern regions I have found a country more thickly inhabited by people and animals than our Europe or Asia or Africa."

Thus he wrote privately to a friend in Italian. It was translated into Latin, printed and published in Paris as a little four-leaved tractlet, and eagerly read. Amerigo Vespucci had discovered another world beyond the equator, they said. It was not the land of Columbus, but altogether something new and strange.

For the first time the vague idea of a new continent began to take shape in the public mind.

Vespucci's voyages were widely read; and in the year 1507 we find these words in a little old geography book written at this time to tell people all that was known about the world. The earth was divided into three parts, says the little old book. "But now," it goes on, "these parts have been more thoroughly explored, and another fourth part has been discovered by Amerigo Vespucci; wherefore," adds the author, "I do not see what is rightly to hinder us from calling it America—the land of Americus—after its discoverer Americus."

The name was taken up, and in the maps of the time we find a vague piece of land somewhere away in the Atlantic Ocean called America.

It was left for others to discover that the land of Columbus, of Cabot, and of Amerigo Vespucci, were one and the same.

CHAPTER 42

DISCOVERY OF THE PACIFIC

"This day is full of glorious victory,
Echoes of conquest whisper from afar
In every wave of the remembering sea."
—H. BEGBIE.

AMONG all the wonderful stories in the discovery of
America there is none more thrilling than that of the
Spaniard Balboa, the stowaway, who found the great
Pacific Ocean lying beyond the newly discovered
country.

All eyes were now turned towards America.
Ship after ship still sailed westward. Still no one had
as yet crossed the mainland, no one knew for certain
that a great sea washed the farther coast of the new
world which lay between Europe and Asia, Spain
and China.

Among others who left Spain to settle in the
new colony of Hayti, founded by Columbus, was
Vasco Nuñez de Balboa. He had not been a
successful tiller of the soil, and before long he found
himself in debt. By law no debtor was allowed to
leave the country, so Balboa had been forced to see

expedition after expedition depart from Hayti for adventure and conquest, leaving him always behind.

One day a ship sailed away from the new colony. On board were soldiers, sailors, arms, and food. In the midst of the cargo stood a barrel, supposed to contain food. But it contained a live man instead. The ship was well out to sea, when the stowaway crawled out of his barrel and appeared on deck. It was Balboa, the Spanish knight. The captain was very angry, and threatened to land him on a desert island. But Balboa's entreaties touched him, and he was allowed to sail on with the rest of them. They were close to land when the ship ran upon a rock, and was very soon dashed to pieces.

Balboa—a "man who was never deterred"— now rose to the occasion. He led the shipwrecked party to a friendly Indian village near Darien. The Spaniards were on the narrow neck of land now known as the isthmus of Panama, which joins North and South America, though they knew it not. Arrived here, Balboa deposed the captain, sent him back to Hayti, and made himself governor of the little colony. He explored the neighbourhood, finding Indian villages rich in gold and the chiefs ready to give information about the new country.

One day some gold was being weighed out to the Spaniards, who were quarrelling over the quantity, when the prince, who was disgusted with their behaviour, dashed the gold from the scales, crying, "What is this, Christians? is it for such a little thing that you quarrel? If you have such a love of gold that to obtain it you harass the peaceful nations of these lands, I will show you a country where you may fulfill your desires. You will have to fight your way with great kings, among them one whose country is distant from our country six suns."

The prince pointed away to the south, where, he said, lay a great sea. There were sails and oars on the sea, and if they crossed it they would find a land of great riches, where people drank out of golden cups.

A feverish longing to find this great sea seized Balboa, but he could not reach it with so few men. So he sent a messenger back to the King of Spain to beg for help. Storms raged in the Atlantic Ocean, and it was eight months before the messenger reached Spain. Then he found that the captain deposed by Balboa had been before him and poisoned the king's mind against his subject. Something of this reached the ears of Balboa in distant Darien. He felt his dismissal would come, and he must find the great new sea first.

So he collected about two hundred men and started on his perilous expedition. Making friends of the Indians he met, Balboa reached at last the high range of mountains which divided him from the other coast. Led by native guides the Spaniards struggled up the steep sides, up and ever upwards. At last the guides signed to Balboa that he was near the top. He bade his men sit down. He must be alone to see that great sight for which his soul had yearned. It was all true. As he reached the summit of

Balboa looked down on the Pacific.

the peak he looked down over the vast Pacific Ocean, bathed in the brilliant light of a tropical sun. He was the first man from the old world who had seen it. Falling on his knees, he thanked God, for that he had discovered the Sea of the South.

Then he beckoned up his men.

"You see here, gentlemen and children mine," he said, when they had gathered at the top and were feasting their eyes on the view before them, "the end of our labours."

It was not unlike the moment when Hannibal stood on the top of the snowy Alps and pointed to his men the land of Italy lying below in the sunshine.

Then, having sung the "Te Deum," they made a cross, heaped up stones, and took formal possession of the sea and all that was in it in the name of the King of Spain. After this they made their way down the farther side of the mountain to the beach. Finding two native canoes on the shore, two men sprang in and pushed off, crying aloud that they were the first Europeans to sail on the new sea, while Balboa waded in up to his hips, sword in hand, to take possession of the sea for Spain.

Thus on September 29, 1513, was completed the first discovery of the Pacific Ocean. The discoverer, Balboa, was made governor of the new sea, but five years later he was beheaded by one who was jealous of his powers.

CHAPTER 43

MAGELLAN'S GREAT PLAN

"They were the first that ever burst
Into that silent sea."
—COLERIDGE.

BEFORE relating how Magellan started off on his voyage round the world, let us turn back for a moment and see how former discoverers had prepared the way for this wonderful voyage.

It was just one hundred years since Prince Henry of Portugal had set up his watch-tower on the bleak southern coast of Spain, despatching ship after ship to explore the western coast of Africa. Forty-six years later the equator was passed; another forty years and Bartholomew Diaz had sighted the mysterious Cape at the south of Africa, which was discovered by Vasco da Gama eleven years later on his way to India.

So much for the Portuguese voyages to the East.

Meanwhile Columbus was sailing to the West in the service of Spain, discovering islands off the coast of North America, to be followed by Cabot to Newfoundland, Cabral to Brazil, and Amerigo Vespucci to the mouth of the great river La Plata, to the south of Brazil. All these explorers had touched the coast of America at different points, fondly dreaming that it was the coast of Asia.

Other ideas were, as we have seen, slowly taking shape, when Balboa discovered the great sea on the far side of America, thus enlarging the geography of the world.

There was a young Portuguese sailor called Magellan. He had sailed with Albuquerque in the expedition to Goa, after which he had accompanied him to the islands beyond India, now known as the East Indies, in the first European ships which had ventured beyond Ceylon.

Here is a story told of Magellan, which shows him to be made of the stern stuff of heroes. While the ships were preparing to take in a cargo of pepper and ginger from the city of Malacca, the king was plotting for their destruction. The commander of the expedition was sitting on the quarterdeck of his flag-ship, deep in a game of chess, which the dark faces of the natives watched intently. No one suspected them of treason. Ashore, the houses rose one above another on the hillside, while the tall tower of the citadel glistened in the September sunshine.

From time to time the natives on the shore and on board glanced to the top of the tower, expecting every moment to see the puff of smoke which would tell them to fall upon the foreigners and put them to death. But the secret had just leaked out. Information reached the nearest ships, and suddenly the Portuguese sailors began chasing the natives from their decks. Magellan sprang into a boat, and made for the flag-ship, shouting "Treason! treason!" He was just in time to save the chess-loving commander.

Meanwhile one Serrano, in charge of the cargo, was being pursued by the light skiffs of the Malay natives. He was struggling against fearful odds, when Magellan rowed up and joined battle with such strength and fury that he saved Serrano. The European guns soon did the rest, and the Malays attacked no more. This was the beginning of a devoted friendship between Magellan and Serrano, out of which grew perhaps the most wonderful voyage ever related in history.

Soon after this Magellan returned to Portugal. For seven long years and more he had fought with wind and wave,—he had suffered the hardships which belonged to the life of a sailor in those early days of navigation. He was longing to be off again, to explore farther among those islands beyond India. Dreams of finding his way to them by sailing westwards past the New World of Columbus never left him. There must be some strait through which he could reach the Indian Ocean and the Spice Islands, as some of these East India islands were called.

He laid his plan before the King of Portugal, but he refused to listen or help. Magellan then asked whether he might go and lay his scheme before some other master.

"You can do as you please," answered the king.

Upon this Magellan desired to kiss his hand at parting, but the king would not offer it.

As Columbus, Cabot, and Vespucci had done before him, Magellan now passed from Portugal into Spain. He soon found favour in the eyes of Charles V., the boy-king of Spain, who ordered an expedition to be fitted out under his command. Away into the great South Sea, discovered so lately by Balboa, Magellan was to sail. His scheme was not unlike that of Columbus: his dream was to be realised yet more fully than that of the famous discoverer of America.

"Sail to the West and the East will be found."

CHAPTER 44

MAGELLAN'S STRAITS

"Beneath the southern stars' cold gleam, he braves
And stems the whirls of land-surrounded waves;
For ever sacred to the hero's name,
These foaming straits shall bear his deathless fame."
—CAMOENS.

IT was on September 20, 1519, that Magellan's little fleet put out to sea. There were five ships, all small, all old, and the worse for wear. The flag-ship was the Trinidad, though it was not the largest; the smallest ship was commanded by another Serrano, the brother of Magellan's friend, who was still in the East Indies. One was called the Victoria. Little did they think that she alone would struggle back to tell the tale of the wonderful voyage round the world,— she alone, and without her commander Magellan. Some two hundred and eighty men sailed with the fleet—a medley crew of Spaniards and Portuguese, Italians, French, Germans, Greeks, one Englishman, and some black men.

But the King of Portugal was determined that the expedition smiled on by the young King of Spain should not succeed; and the seeds of mutiny were sown among the captains, who actually sailed out of port with treason in their hearts. Though this came to the ears of the commander, yet "be they true men or false, I will fear them not," said Magellan; "I will do my appointed work."

It was three months before they reached the coast of Brazil, in South America. Great Atlantic storms had driven the frail ships out of their course, water had grown scarce, food ran short, and mutiny was brewing. The Spaniards whispered among themselves that the Portuguese commander was not loyal. One day the captain of one of the ships came on board the Trinidad and faced Magellan with threats and insults. He was not a little astonished when Magellan—a strong man with fierce black eyes—seized him and had him bound in irons and sent on board another ship as a prisoner. This firm conduct on the part of the commander quieted matters for a time. They sailed on south to the river La Plata, and satisfied themselves that it was a river and no strait. On they went, coasting ever south and looking for some opening which should lead them into the great South Sea seen by Balboa six years before.

The cold now became intense, so that, finding a sheltered harbour at last and plenty of fish, Magellan anchored for the winter months. It was Easter time, when another mutiny, long smouldering, burst forth in its full fury. The hardships of the voyage had been intense, the terrific Atlantic storms had strained the worn-out ships. The

Spaniards felt they had done enough. But, like Vasco da Gama. the commander was firm. They had put their hands to the plough, there must be no turning back.

It was Easter Day, when two of the Spanish captains boarded one of the other ships, seized its loyal captain, put him in irons, and handed round a generous supply of food. With three ships now in their hands, it seemed easy enough to capture the flag-ship, murder Magellan, and seize the faithful Serrano. But Magellan heard of their design. He sent a messenger with five men bearing concealed arms to summon one of the traitor captains on board the flagship.

"I am not to be caught thus," smiled the Spanish captain, as he read the command and shook his head. As he refused, Magellan's messenger drew his dagger and stabbed him. He fell dead on the deck of his ship. The crew surrendered at once to Magellan's brother-in-law, who now took command of the ship. Magellan blockaded the two remaining ships in the harbour. One of the captains was then beheaded, the other being kept in chains till the fleet sailed off once more, when he was put ashore and left to his fate. Such prompt measures put down mutiny for the rest of the voyage, and once more the ships sailed on their way.

It was now August, in the year 1520, nearly a year since they had left home; but it was not till October that they at last found the bay for which they were searching. With head winds and bad weather the ships fought their way inch by inch between broken land and islands, with strong currents running. In this way a month passed by. The crews begged to turn back. They were riding to destruction.

"If we have to eat the leather on the ship's yards, yet will we go on," answered the brave Magellan.

His words came truer than he knew, for later on, broken down with famine and sickness, they actually did eat the leather on the yards.

At last came a day when they reached a cape beyond which lay the open sea—Balboa's Sea of the South. It was the end of the straits through which they had fought for five long hard weeks; and, says the old story, "when the captain Magellan was past the strait and saw the way open to the other main sea, he was so glad thereof that for joy the tears fell from his eyes."

The broad expanse of calm waters looked peaceful to his tired eyes after the heavy storms through which he had passed, and he called the still sea before him the "Pacific Ocean," which name it bears to-day.

CHAPTER 45

ROUND THE WORLD

"The far-famed ship Victoria men shall sight
Anchored in safest waters by Seville,
When she had girdled ocean-plain profound,
And circled earth in one continuous round."
—CAMOENS.

IT was the 28th of November 1520, when three ships sailed out into the open sea. Two had already deserted, and basely made for home to spread ill reports about the stout-hearted Magellan.

They now sailed northward along the far coast of South America to escape the intense cold. The violent sudden tempests of the Atlantic had given place to steady winds, which drove them gently over the calm surface of the Pacific Ocean. This lasted for three months and twenty days. But during this time their sufferings were intense. Once more a Sea of Darkness must be crossed. The brave hearts despaired as day after day passed away, week after week, month after month, and their straining eyes could catch no sight of land. As they sailed on and on over the immense waste of waters, the great size of the world began to dawn on them. It was so much larger than any one had ever imagined. They had thought on leaving the shores of America that they would soon find the coast of Asia or India.

All December and January they sailed on. Daily their sufferings became more intense. The old historian tells us the heartrending details.

"Having consumed all their biscuits and other victuals," he says, "they fell into such necessity that they were forced to eat the biscuit powder that remained, now full of worms. They did eat skins and pieces of leather which were folded about certain great ropes of the ships. But these skins being made very hard by reason of the sun, rain, and wind, they hung them by a cord in the sea for the space of four or five days to soften them. By reason of the famine and unclean feeding, some of their gums grew so over their teeth that they died."

Indeed nineteen died and thirty more lay too ill to do any work. Still they sailed on over this everlasting stretch of water—vast beyond all knowing. Still that iron will of the commander never bent. With resolute eyes Magellan gazed westward for that land that he knew they must reach sooner or later, for the world, he knew, was round.

At last, after ninety-eight days of weary sailing, they came upon some islands where they could get fresh vegetables and fruit, and end their acute sufferings. After ten days' refreshment they left the islands, and sailed on in search of more land. They soon reached another group, which were afterwards named the Philippine Islands, after Philip of Spain, who was born six years after their discovery.

Though no Europeans had been here before, yet traders from China were here; and Magellan soon realised the importance of the place. He must be near the famous Spice Islands, too, for the natives brought spice to exchange, as well as bananas and cocoa-nuts.

With the good supply of food the sick sailors soon grew better; and for some time Magellan cruised about the islands, making friends as well as Christians of the natives. The Easter services were performed on one of the islands with great ceremony, a cross and crown of thorns was presented to the native king, to be set up on the highest mountain in the island, that all might see and worship.

Thus April passed away in teaching the natives, trading, and establishing the power of Spain everywhere.

But on one island his religious enthusiasm carried Magellan too far. Deciding to subdue a troublesome chief, Magellan landed on one of the islands. It was early dawn on the morning of April 27, 1521. He at once sent a message to the king to beg him to pay tribute to Spain, or he should learn how lances wounded. The answer was defiant. If the Spaniards had lances, the islanders had reeds and stakes hardened by fire.

With forty-eight armed men Magellan stepped ashore, to be met by hundreds and thousands of natives. The fight was desperate and against fearful odds. Again and again Magellan was wounded, until at last, says the old historian who fought by his side all through that last day,—"at last the Indians threw themselves upon him with iron-pointed bamboo spears and every weapon they had and ran him through,—our mirror, our light, our comforter, our true guide,—until they killed him."

So died Magellan, in a miserable skirmish, at the last. With a dauntless courage, in the face of tremendous odds, he had accomplished his work. He had sailed westward over the unknown part of the ocean to a part already reached by Europeans going eastward, thus proving once and for ever that the world was round. The foaming straits at the foot of South America will ever bear his name, which is one of the most famous in the history of discovery.

And who took home the great news?

The little ship Victoria alone. On the 16th May, with starvation thinning her ranks, one mast gone, her timbers strained and worn, she cleared the Cape of Good Hope on her homeward way, and a friendly current bore her over the equator. So starving were the sailors—of whom there were but eighteen left—that they had to stop at the Cape de Verde Islands to recruit. And it was not till September 8 that the welcome shores of Spain hove in sight, and the famine-stricken Spaniards stepped ashore to tell the story of their three years' voyage. It was a story without equal in its sufferings and misery, its failure and success,—a story without equal in the annals of history, for it told of the first circumnavigation of the globe by Magellan.

CHAPTER 46

THE FINDING OF MEXICO

"In later years a time will come when ocean shall
relax his bars, and a vast territory shall appear."
—SENECA (died 67 A.D.)

WE now come to one of the most romantic chapters
in the world's history—the conquest of Mexico by
Hernando Cortes, and the tragic end of Mexico's
native king, Montezuma.

A new and glorious world had been thrown
open. No longer did the Spanish sailors recoil with
horror at the thought of the dark and stormy waters
of the broad Atlantic. There was treasure beyond.
Was it not a land of gold and pearls? Ship after ship
sailed across in safety, always making for Hayti or
Cuba, the West Indies of Columbus. From these
centres the Spaniards sailed to unknown coasts, and
wandered about strange new countries.

One day in the year 1518, some Spaniards,
sailing west from Cuba, landed on soil and met
natives, whom they at once recognised as different
to any they had seen before. They were astonished to
see houses built of stone and lime, the soil cultivated,

gold ornaments on the people, and delicately made cotton garments. They gave the Spaniards rich treasures of jewels, and golden ornaments of wondrous form and workmanship. Surely here was a rich country, a country which must be conquered for Spain as soon as possible.

A messenger was sent off to the mother country with news of this rich discovery and its treasures of gold. The king—no longer Ferdinand—was pleased; and he soon selected a rich subject, Fernando Cortes, to take charge of an expedition to this new country, which the natives called Mexico. Cortes had already been to Cuba. He was delighted at the prospect of his new work. He received his instructions from the King of Spain. He was to convert the Indians of Mexico to the Christian faith; he was to impress on them the greatness of Spain, to which country they should in future look for protection, showing their good will by presents of pearls, gold, and precious jewels. All was to be done for the service of God and the king.

On the 18th of November 1518, Cortes set sail from Spain. His banner was a red cross set amid flames of blue and white, on a background of black velvet and gold, bearing the motto: "Friends, let us follow the cross, and under this sign we shall conquer."

Arrived at Cuba he mustered his forces. There were one hundred and ten sailors, five hundred and fifty-three soldiers, two hundred natives from Cuba, together with ten heavy guns and sixteen horses. A small enough force for the conquest of Mexico. Before embarking, Cortes addressed his men.

"I hold out to you a glorious prize," he said, "but it is to be won by incessant toil. Be true to me, as I will be true to you. You are few in number but strong in resolution, and if this does not fail, the Almighty, who has never deserted the Spaniard in his contest with the heathen, will shield you, for your cause is a just one, and you are to fight under the banner of the cross."

With great enthusiasm for their leader Cortes, they crossed over to the coast of Mexico. It was April 21—Good Friday—in the year 1519, when Cortes landed his little force on the very spot where now stands the modern town of Vera Cruz. Little did he think, as he set foot on this desolate beach, that one day a flourishing city should arise to be a market of Eastern trade and the commercial capital of New Spain.

Natives now flocked to the shore, bringing presents to the Spanish general,—fine cottons, feather-work cloaks, and ornaments of gold,—till the men grew enthusiastic over the riches of Mexico. Cortes asked if he could see the ruler of this rich country. He told them all about the great King of Spain, who had sent him thither. That there should be another ruler in the world as great as their great emperor Montezuma surprised the natives not a little. They must go and tell him all this news.

Then a curious thing happened. One native took a pencil and sketched, on a piece of canvas or 'cotton, pictures of the Spaniards—their dress, their shining helmets, their pointed beards, their arms. Nothing was lost on these Mexican painters. They drew the ships—the water-houses as they called them—with their dark hulls and snow-white sails, as they swung lazily at anchor in the bay. To impress them yet more deeply, Cortes ordered his soldiers to go through some of their military exercises on horseback. The clever management of the fiery horses on the wet sand, the shrill blast of the trumpets, the shining swords, filled the natives with surprise. But when they heard the thunder of the guns, and saw the smoke and flame of the cannon, they were filled with terror.

They must indeed go and tell their great Montezuma of all they had seen and heard, and they would bring the Spaniards word again whether he would grant Cortes an audience.

CHAPTER 47

MONTEZUMA

"The ports ye shall not enter,
The roads ye shall not tread."
—KIPLING.

THE natives went back to Montezuma at Mexico. They showed him the pictures of the Spaniards, and he was sore troubled. He had reigned over his country for sixteen years. A sad, severe, somewhat melancholy man, he had a great idea of his own importance. He never set foot on the ground in public, but was carried on the shoulders of noblemen. Whenever he alighted, they laid down rich tapestry for him to walk on. No man, under the rank of a knight, might look on his face. He never put on the same garment twice, he never ate or drank out of the same dish more than once. The people looked on him as a god.

Cortes now resolved to pay him a visit in his capital, and he began quietly to prepare for the journey. First he built the little town of Vera Cruz— the True Cross—on the sea-shore as a basis of future operations. It was dawning on him, too, that

215

there were timid souls in the camp; he did not feel sure they would wait for his return from Mexico, so he made up his mind to do a desperate thing. He destroyed the ships in the harbour of Vera Cruz, all save one. The news created a panic among the Spaniards, now cut off from home and friends. They were on a hostile shore, a mere handful of men against a powerful kingdom. Murmurs grew louder and louder. Mutiny threatened. Cortes spoke: "If there be any so cowardly as to shrink from sharing the dangers of this glorious enterprise, let them go home. There is one ship left. Let them take it and return to Cuba. They can tell how they deserted their commander and their comrades, and wait till we return laden with spoils from Mexico."

They had put their hands to the plough, there must be no turning back. Enthusiasm for their leader revived, his banner should lead them to victory. Not a man stirred away as the air rang with shouts, "To Mexico! To Mexico!"

The march was long and tedious, and it was three months before Cortes and his army reached the capital. With the first faint streak of dawn on the 8th of November, Montezuma's beautiful city of Mexico came into sight. "Forward, soldiers, the Holy Cross is our banner, and under that sign we shall conquer," cried the commander.

With beating hearts and trumpets sounding, the Spaniards strained their eyes over the gorgeous sight before them. The sacred flames on the altars, dimly seen through the mists of the early morning, showed the site of temples and towers. The palace itself was soon seen in the glorious morning sunshine as it rose and poured over the wondrous valley.

Mexico was one of the most beautiful cities of the world.

"Who shall describe Mexico!" cries the enthusiastic historian; "only one who has seen all the wonders of the world."

No wonder the Spaniards looked with envy on the fair city; no wonder they longed for the wealth, the boundless wealth, of this wondrous land. At the walls of the city Cortes heard that, after all, Montezuma was coming out to meet him; and true enough the Spaniards soon saw, amid a crowd of nobles, the royal chair, blazing with gold. It was borne on the shoulders of barefooted knights, who walked with downcast eyes. Over the king was a canopy of feather-work, powdered with jewels and fringed with silver. As the king alighted, the Spaniards could see his cloak was sprinkled with precious stones and pearls; on his feet were golden sandals, on his head were plumes of royal green.

Cortes explained his mission. He spoke to the king of his mission—to teach the heathen of Christ. He begged Montezuma to give up his idols and strange gods and to abstain from human sacrifices. The king refused. Cortes saw that as long as Montezuma sat on the throne of Mexico no conversion of the people could take place. They must dethrone the king. In vain to argue with him: he was resolute.

"Why do we waste time on this barbarian?" he cried. "Let us seize him, and if he resists, plunge our swords into his body."

The fierce tone of the Spaniards alarmed the king. If death were the alternative, then he must go. He looked at the stern faces and iron forms of these strange Spaniards, and he felt that his hour was come.

One day the Mexicans held a great festival. Montezuma was not allowed to take part in it, but six hundred of his people, decked out in mantles of feather-work and collars of gold, were dancing their sacred dance, when a party of Spaniards rushed on them with drawn swords, and without mercy or pity slew them to a man.

Then the long-pent-up fury of the people burst forth in a great cry for revenge, and they rushed upon the Spaniards. A frantic fight took place, until the Spaniards begged Montezuma to intercede. Dressing himself for the last time in his royal robes, the king mounted one of the battlements of his palace. His mantle of blue and white flowed from his shoulders, held together by a rich clasp of green. Emeralds set in gold shone on his dress. His feet were shod in golden sandals, on his head shone the crown of Mexico. As he appeared, the clang of war and fierce cries were hushed, and a death-like silence reigned. All eyes were cast down. Montezuma the king was among them again.

"Why do I see my people here in arms?" he cried to the crowds below; "is it to release your king? Your king is not a prisoner: these strangers are my guests. Return to your homes, then, and lay down your arms."

Murmurs ran through the crowd. Was Montezuma, then, the friend of these hated Spaniards? Did he not mind all the insults and injuries that had been heaped on their unhappy nation? Their fierce Mexican blood boiled.

"Base! Woman! Coward!" Such words they flung at the unhappy king. Then a cloud of stones and arrows were aimed at the solitary figure standing aloft on the turret of his palace, and Montezuma fell senseless to the ground. He was borne away by his faithful knights; but he had nothing more to live for. He had tasted the last drop in his bitter cup,—his own people had turned against him. A few days later he died.

Mexico was no longer a safe place for the Spaniards, and Cortes left the city the following night, hoping to escape under cover of darkness. But the Mexicans were not asleep. They fell upon the Spaniards as they crept noiselessly forth, killed numbers, and took the gold they were carrying away with them. When morning dawned and Cortes gazed at this shattered army, and missed the familiar faces of those who had braved so much for him, he sat down upon a rock, buried his face in his hands, and wept.

CHAPTER 48

SIEGE AND FALL OF MEXICO

"So shall inferior eyes,
That borrow their behaviour from the great,
Grow great by your example, and put on
The dauntless spirit of resolution."
—SHAKSPERE.

NOT for one moment, however, did the brave Cortes flinch in his purpose of taking Mexico. The "melancholy night," as it has since been called in history, had wrought sad havoc with his troops; but such was the determination of the man that, ten months later, he was ready to besiege the city of Mexico. It was April 28, 1521, the day after Magellan had died in the Philippine Islands, though Cortes knew it not, for news travelled very slowly in those days.

The story of the siege of Mexico is one of the most striking in the world's history. The dauntless heroism of the Mexicans in their wonderful defence was equalled only by the determination of the Spaniards to suffer no defeat at their hands.

With extra supplies of men and ships from Spain, Cortes marched to the great city on the waters. Before long, on the great lake surrounding the city, sailed the Spanish ships, with music sounding and the royal flag of Spain proudly floating in the air. The ships, like snowy sea-birds, bounded over the waters, until a shout of admiration broke from the Mexicans. Then guns roared from the shore, and the stern Spaniards felt that success was at last going to crown their efforts.

Once more Cortes roused them to enthusiasm.

"I have taken the last step," he cried; "I have brought you to the goal for which you have so long panted, the capital from which you were driven with so much disgrace. We are fighting the battles of the Faith—fighting for our honour, for riches, for revenge. I have brought you face to face with your foe: it is for you to do the rest."

A thundering chorus of voices declared that every man would do his duty under such a leader as Ferdinand Cortes.

So by water and land they attacked the beautiful city and assaulted the brave defenders. It was a time of unceasing toil, almost beyond the strength of the stubborn Spaniards. Through long, wet, cold nights, and scorched by the tropical sun by day, they had to stand at their posts. Their sufferings were great indeed, but their firm resolve to take the city was greater.

Meanwhile famine was striding through the heart of Mexico. The stores of the Mexicans were exhausted. They had eaten all the Spaniards they could take, as well as rats, lizards, and other reptiles; but their hatred of the enemy was undying, and, animated by despair, they fought on. Cortes sent message after message to urge surrender. The game was up, the fair city was crumbling into ruins.

"Spain shall take your city under her protection," ended the proposal.

The eye of the young king—Montezuma's nephew—kindled. His dark cheek flushed with sudden anger as he listened to such a message. He called his wise men together.

"Peace is good," they said, "but not with these white men. Better, if need be, give up our lives at once for our country than drag on in slavery and suffering among strangers."

"Then," cried the young king, "let no man henceforth talk of surrender. We can at least die like warriors."

But their strength was not equal to their spirit. Their very streets were full of dead and dying men.

"A man could not set his foot down," said Cortes afterwards, "except on the corpse of an Indian."

Death was everywhere. Calm and courageous in the midst of dead and dying, his fair capital in ruins before his very eyes, the young king stood firm. In vain Cortes sought an interview to persuade him that his noblest path was now to surrender. Messengers came and went, but the young king refused to see Cortes.

"Go, then," cried Cortes at last, impatiently, "and prepare your countrymen for death: their hour is come."

So the ruler of Mexico was captured.

"Better despatch me with this and rid me of life at once," he cried desperately, drawing his sword as Cortes came forward to receive him with studied courtesy. The proud bearing of the young Mexican was worthy the spirit of an ancient Roman.

"Fear not," replied Cortes, "you shall be treated with all honour. You have defended your capital like a brave warrior: a Spaniard knows how to respect valour even in an enemy."

So the Spaniards conquered Mexico at last. Soon a new city rose on the ruins of the last, still more beautiful and still more important, until the old writers cried in their ecstasy: "Europe cannot boast a single city as fair and rich as Mexico."

CHAPTER 49

CONQUEST OF PERU

"Not to be wearied, not to be deterred,
Not to be overcome."
        —SOUTHEY (on Pizarro).

THE dazzling conquest of Mexico gave a new impulse to American discovery.

"If gold is what you prize so much, that you are willing to leave your distant homes and even risk life itself," the Indian prince had said to Balboa, "I can tell you of a land where they drink out of golden vessels, and gold is as cheap as iron in your own country."

He spoke of Peru, on the western coast of South America, washed by the waters of the Pacific Ocean. Among those who heard him was one Pizarro, who as a young man had climbed the steep mountain with Balboa, and looked his fill on the hitherto unknown waters of the Pacific Ocean.

But it was not till three years after Magellan had sailed across the Pacific Ocean, and five since Cortes had conquered Mexico, that Pizarro got his chance and started off from the little port of Panama in search of the golden kingdom of Peru.

This first expedition was a dismal failure; and after untold hardships Pizarro returned to Panama in a sorry state. Still undaunted in spirit, he again started forth. The land of gold was farther away than he had imagined, the coast was stormy and inhospitable, the natives unfriendly.

At last, however, an expedition was fitted out, and guided by the clever pilot Ruiz, who was well experienced in the navigation of the Pacific, they reached the island of Gallo, near the equator. Here they determined to wait, and send back for more troops from Panama, as there was clearly fighting to be done on the coast of Peru. But this proposal caused a great outcry.

"What," faltered the faint-hearted, "are we to be left in this obscure spot to die of hunger?"

What did they care for lands of gold: they only wanted to go home. But the ships sailed away for help, and Pizarro was left alone on the far-off island with his discontented crew. They survived on crabs and shell-fish, picked up on the shore, till the two welcome ships returned well laden with food and men. By this time Pizarro's men had made up their minds to return to Panama at all costs. Pizarro was determined to go on. Drawing his sword one day, he traced a line on the sand from east to west. Then turning to the south, he cried—

"Friends and comrades, on that side are toil, hunger, nakedness, the drenching storm, desertion, and death; on this side ease and pleasure. There lies Peru with its riches: here Panama and its poverty. Choose, each man, what best becomes a brave Spaniard. For my part, I go south."

Saying this, he stepped across the line. The brave pilot and twelve others followed him, while the rest turned their faces homewards.

The old historian speaks with enthusiasm of this little band of men, who in the face of difficulties unequalled in history, with death rather than riches for their reward, never deserted their leader in the hour of his greatest need—an example of loyalty for all future ages.

It was the crisis of Pizarro's life. The little band now sailed southwards, 600 miles south of the equator, touching at various points along the coast. After a year and a half's absence they found themselves once more in the port of Panama, telling their eager listeners that they had indeed found the land of gold, and they had only come back to fit out a new expedition to go and conquer it.

Pizarro now returned to Spain, where he obtained leave from the king to attempt the conquest of Peru, of which he was named Governor, on a promise to pay the king one-fifth part of all the treasure he might get. In February 1531 he landed in Peru with two hundred men and fifty horses. He at once marched south along the coast, built a town, which he called San Miguel, as head-quarters, and learned more of the country he meant to conquer.

Pizarro then started off on his inland journey, to find the monarch, or Inca as he was called, of these parts. It was September 1532 when he began his great march for the Peruvian city of Caxamalca, where the king was to be found. It was a daring enterprise, for between the Spaniards and the old city of Peru rose a great mountain-range, which numbered some of the highest peaks in the whole world. This range was known as the Andes. After a few days' march they saw the stupendous range rising before them, their crests of everlasting snow glittering amid the clouds.

It needed some courage to plunge across those lonely mountain ways to the capital of the Incas.

"Let each man take heart and go forward like a good soldier," cried Pizarro.

"Lead on, wherever thou thinkest best," shouted his devoted followers; "we will follow."

Scrambling up rocks, winding along narrow ledges with yawning chasms below, always leading their horses by the bridle, the brave Spaniards struggled through the very heart of the mountains. At the top they looked down on the little old city of Caxamalca glittering in the sunshine.

Meanwhile the news had reached the Inca that white bearded strangers had come up from the sea, clad in shining array, riding upon "unearthly monsters" and wielding deadly thunderbolts. The ruler of Peru at once sent messengers, laden with presents, to make friends with these strangers.

As the conquerors neared the city, the Inca was carried on his golden litter to meet them.

A solitary white man came forth. It was the Spanish priest, who proceeded to give him a long account of Bible history from the Creation to the call of St Peter, begging him at the same time to accept a Spanish Bible, and thus acknowledge the power of Spain. As the Inca hurled the Bible from him, a number of armed Spaniards rushed out of the houses surrounding the market-place, where they had been in hiding, seized the terrified Inca, and slew his followers. Pizarro had the Inca shut up in a room till his fate should be decided. Making a mark on the wall, as high as his hand would reach, the poor deposed ruler offered the Spaniards as ransom for his life gold enough to fill the room up to the height he had marked. Pizarro accepted the offer, but afterwards he easily put the Inca to death.

A year later Pizarro entered the city of Cuzco, the capital of Peru. The city was full of treasure, as he had expected. There were figures of pure gold and planks of solid silver. The women wore sandals of gold, and their dresses glittered with beads of gold.

So the "Children of the Sun" entered into possession of the old town of Cuzco, and the conquest of golden Peru was practically complete.

When the loads of gold from this rich country and the wonderful tales of adventure reached Spain, there was such excitement as had hardly been felt since Columbus had returned from his first voyage across the Sea of Darkness. Again Spaniards flocked across the seas to the New World, and ships plied between Spain and Peru. Pizarro himself was made a Marquis, and his name was on every lip, for had he not surmounted every obstacle to win this great country for Spain?

CHAPTER 50

A GREAT AWAKENING

"And the voices of the day
Are heard across the voices of the dark."
—TENNYSON.

LET us now gather up the threads of our story of the Middle Ages, and see how men's eyes were opened to all the beauty and the glory of the world around them.

The Dark Ages had passed away for ever, the gloom of the fourteenth century would never return. The tide of barbarianism had swept over the smiling fields of Europe like a torrent of mud, quenching all life and joy.

But the seeds were still there; and as time passed on they were to spring up again through the mud, to become yet more beautiful, yet more glorious than they were before.

The world had been asleep, and now its time for awakening had come. Partly it came with Christianity. The Crusades showed the spirit that was spreading through Europe, as Christ became more and more a world power, and the eyes of men were turned to the Holy City away in distant Syria. The great empire of Rome had fallen, but a far grander empire of the world had arisen from its ashes.

As Dante began to sing, the world was "turning in its sleep." Its long slumber was disturbed by broken fragments of dream, by gleams of light, by voices in the night, bidding it throw off its world-fetters and venture forth into the radiance of the morning light.

One of the first to awake had been Prince Henry of Portugal. Over the Sea of Darkness he had shed a light, until the whole ocean was slowly revealed in the brightness of the day.

The awakening was slow. Gradually men ventured forth, until the Portuguese sailors had doubled the Cape of Good Hope and anchored their merchant fleets in the harbours of India, Columbus added a new world to the old, Magellan proved beyond dispute that the world was round.

Meanwhile Copernicus had discovered new wonders in the heavens, and the invention of printing had placed the new wonders in the hands of all. So this sudden contact with new wonders, new lands, and new creeds opened men's eyes to new and glorious possibilities.

But there was something else which helped Europe to awake and claim her manhood again. Constantinople—the old capital of the East—had fallen into the hands of the Turks. This important city, away on the Golden Horn, had been the centre of learning for centuries, and there had been stored the masterpieces and art treasures of the old world. Now a general flight of her scholars, her artists, her poets, her philosophers, had to take place. And whither should they flee save to the shores of Italy, to the little city under the Tuscan hills, to the old home of Dante—Florence?

And so the poetry of Homer and the philosophy of Plato woke to life again in that little city by the river Arno, which was ever the home of learning and art. Here the great thoughts and writings of the Greeks were translated into other languages. The long silence of centuries was broken at last. The ships from Venice brought back manuscripts from the East as the most precious part of their cargo.

Scholars from Germany, England, France, flocked over the snowy Alps to learn Greek, so that they might carry back the new learning to their own countries.

"Greece has crossed the Alps," cried one, on hearing a Greek translation of one of the old masters read in Germany.

"I have given up my whole soul to Greek learning," said Erasmus with enthusiasm; "and as soon as I get any money I shall buy Greek books, and then I shall buy some clothes."

So a new and joyous life took hold of Europe. Men had been bound and now they were free. "For the first time they opened their eyes and saw." And what they now saw was the beauty of the world, the glory of learning for learning's sake, the love of all that was good and noble on earth. Each man longed to write more beautiful poems, to paint more beautiful pictures, to build more beautiful houses; and this slow awakening of Europe is one of the most wonderful things in the world's history.

TEACHER'S APPENDIX

Chap.

General Sketch of European History. Freeman.

Europe. Primer. Freeman.

Roman Empire of Second Century. Capes. Epochs of Modern History.

Students' Roman Empire. Bury.

Decline and Fall of the Roman Empire. Gibbons. Students' Edition.

History of Rome. Robinson.

6. *Pliny's Letters.*

Last Days of Pompeii. (Fiction.) Bulwer Lytton.

7. *Meditations of Marcus Aurelius.*

10. *Byzantine Empire.* Oman. (330-1453.) Story of the Nations.

11. *Beginning of the Middle Ages.* (500-1000). Church. Epochs.

The Goths. Bradley. Story of the Nations.

Theodoric the Goth. Hodgkin. Heroes of the Nations.

235

12. *The Dark Ages.* Oman.

13. *King Arthur.* Malory.

    Morte d'Arthur. Tennyson.

14. *Charlemagne.* Hodgkin. Foreign Statesmen Series.

    Charlemagne. Davis. Heroes of the Nations.

    The Franks. Story of the Nations.

15. *The Normans in Europe.* (850-1154.) Johnson. Epochs.

    The Normans. Story of the Nations.

    Hereward the Wake. (Fiction.) Kingsley.

16. *William the Conqueror.* Freeman. Twelve English Statesmen.

    Harold. (Fiction.) Lytton.

    Harold. (Play.) Tennyson.

17. *The Cid.* Campeader. Heroes of the Nations.

    Spain. Story of the Nations.

18. *Crusades.* Cox. Epochs of Modern History.

    Crusades. Story of the Nations.

Jerusalem Delivered. Tasso. Transl. Bohn Library.

19. *Germany.* Baring-Gould. Story of the Nations.

20. *Saladin.* Lane-Poole. Heroes of the Nations.

   Talisman. (Fiction.) Sir W. Scott.

21. *Essays on Chivalry and Romance.* Sir W. Scott.

22. *Venice.* Sonnet by Wordsworth.

   Venice. Story of the Nations.

   Venetian Studies. Horatio Brown.

23. *European Colonies.* Payne. Macmillan's Historical Course.

   Story of Geographical Discovery. Jacobs. Newnes.

   Polo's Voyages and Travels. Bohn Library.

24. *Dante's Vision of Hell, Purgatory, and Paradise.* Transl. Cary.

   Dante in Carlyle's *Heroes and Hero-Worship.*

25. *Joan of Arc.* Heroes of the Nations.

   Maid of Orleans. Schiller. Transl. in Bohn Library.

Short History of English People. Green.

26. *Prince Henry the Navigator.* Heroes of the Nations.

Portugal. Story of the Nations.

The Lusiads. Camoens. Transl. Bohn Library.

30. *South Africa.* Theal. Story of the Nations.

Story of S. Africa. Worsfold. Story of the Empire Series.

32. *Story of India.* Boulger. Story of the Empire Series.

34. *Albuquerque.* Hunter. Rulers of India Series.

35. *Christopher Columbus.* Washington Irving.

36. *The Moors in Spain.* Story of the Nations.

Ferdinand and Isabella. Prescott.

37. *The Conquerors of the New World.* Sir A. Helps.

41. *John Cabot and his Sons.* Beazley. Builders of Greater Britain.

46. *Conquest of Mexico.* Prescott.

49. *Conquest of Peru.* Prescott.

CPSIA information can be obtained
at www.ICGtesting.com
Printed in the USA
LVHW031922030420
652124LV00001B/58